# AROUND THE BOREE LOG

a selection from *Around the Boree Log* and
*The Parish of St Mel's*

# John O'Brien
# AROUND THE BOREE LOG

a selection from *Around the Boree Log* and *The Parish of St Mel's*

*Illustrated by* **Patrick Carroll**

ANGUS
& ROBERTSON
PUBLISHERS

# ACKNOWLEDGMENTS

The poems on pages 18 to 62 are reprinted with permission from John O'Brien: *Around The Boree Log* and the poems on pages 64 to 76 from John O'Brien: *The Parish Of St Mel's*. Both collections are published by Angus & Robertson.

ANGUS & ROBERTSON PUBLISHERS

Unit 4, Eden Park, 31 Waterloo Road,
North Ryde, NSW, Australia 2113, and
16 Golden Square, London W1R 4BN,
United Kingdom

This book is copyright.
Apart from any fair dealing for the
purposes of private study, research,
criticism or review, as permitted
under the Copyright Act, no part may
be reproduced by any process without
written permission. Inquiries should
be addressed to the publishers.

This illustrated edition
first published in Australia
by Angus & Robertson Publishers in 1978
Reprinted 1979, 1980 (twice), 1983, 1986, 1988

© Poems, John O'Brien 1921 © F. A. Mecham 1952, 1954
© Paintings, Patrick Carroll 1978
© John O'Brien Introduction, F. A. Mecham 1978
© Patrick Carroll Introduction, Patrick Carroll 1978
© This illustrated selection, Angus & Robertson Publishers 1978

National Library of Australia
Cataloguing-in-publication data.

O'Brien, John.
   Around the Boree log, and other verse.
   ISBN 0 207 13661 0

   1. Carroll, Patrick, illus. II. Title.
A821'.2

Filmset in Monophoto Bembo
by Asco Trade Typesetting Ltd, Hong Kong
Printed in Singapore

# CONTENTS

*John O'Brien*   6

*Patrick Carroll*   14

Around The Boree Log   18

Peter Nelson's Fiddle   20

The Little Irish Mother   22

Ten Little Steps and Stairs   24

The Old Bush School   26

Six Brown Boxer Hats   28

When The Circus Came To Town   30

The Kookaburras   33

The Trimmin's On The Rosary   34

The Church Upon The Hill   36

St Patrick's Day   38

Said Hanrahan   40

The Altar-Boy   42

At Casey's After Mass   43

Teddo Wells, Deceased   46

Calling To Me   47

Come, Sing Australian Songs To Me!   48

Old Mass Shandrydan   50

The Presbyt'ry Dog   56

Tangmalangaloo   58

Ownerless   60

Laughing Mary   62

Firin' On The Eight   64

Old Sister Paul   67

The Parish Of St Mel's   70

The Durkins   71

Sing Me A Song   72

The Day Th' Inspector Comes   74

The Meeting   75

The Pastor Of St Mel's   76

# JOHN O'BRIEN

When *Around the Boree Log*, by John O'Brien, was first published by Angus and Robertson in 1921 a reviewer from the Melbourne *Age* wrote:

> The writer's familiarity with the devotions of the Church suggests that he may well be one of its immediate servants. But whatever his identity, he has proved his title to a worthy place among Australian poets.

The purpose of this introduction is obviously not to reveal the identity of 'John O'Brien' he is well known to have been Monsignor Patrick Joseph Hartigan, for many years parish priest of Narrandera. Rather it is to give a brief background to the man born at Yass, New South Wales, in 1878 who was destined to take his place among the best sellers of Australian verse.

Hartigan is a Celtic name that was prevalent in the Irish counties of Limerick and Clare. One of the Hartigans was a hero at Clontarf in 1014 A.D. when Brian Boru drove the Danes out of Ireland; another, appropriately enough, was a royal bard.

By 1925, when Father Hartigan endeavoured to trace his ancestry in Lisseycasey, County Clare, the Hartigan name had disappeared from the district. He did discover relatives on the maternal side with the name Trousdell (when his mother came to Australia it had been Townsell). It may earlier have been Townsend—Irish families adopted English names after the siege of Limerick in 1651.

The Australian saga of this branch of the Hartigan family begins in 1864 when Patrick Joseph Snr arrived in Australia from Lisseycasey. He spent a few years as a station book-keeper and storeman at Yass, Southern New South Wales, (Sands' New South Wales Directory for 1867 lists him as being at Hardwicke Station on the Yass Plains, a few miles from the town) and later set up a produce store in Cooma Street, Yass. He

*Father Patrick Hartigan ('John O'Brien') photographed shortly after* **Around the Boree Log** *was first published in 1921. He would have been forty-three years of age.*

married Mary Townsell (also from Lisseycasey) at St Mary's Cathedral, Sydney, on 25 July 1871 and brought her to the home he had acquired in O'Connell Town, Yass. Patrick Joseph was born there on 13 October 1878, the fourth of nine children. Frank, the youngest boy, became a priest of Goulburn diocese (and, when that was divided in 1918, of the newly formed diocese of Wagga); four of the daughters entered Mercy convents; Michael joined the Public Service and married Irene Costello of Lismore; Annie, the youngest girl, after teaching for a few years, married Dick Mecham of Lewisham. John, the eldest, died in infancy.

The earliest glimpse we have of young Patrick, apart from official entries, is a letter preserved at St Patrick's College, Manly, a suburb of Sydney. It was written to the President in January 1892 by Sister Mary Bernard of the Convent of Mercy, Yass:

> There is a very good, smart little boy who is going to some College to complete his studies. His name is Hartigan. I have requested his Mother to send him, if she possibly could, to Manly. She has asked me to write and learn for her particulars as to pension, outfit etc. It is best your reply be addressed to Mr P. Hartigan, O'Connell Town, Yass; he is father of the boy. He has a large family and no one to earn for him yet. If any reduction is made in College fees at Manly, the charity will not be misplaced here. I see the family has to go in for much economy to let the boy away. His sisters with us are giving up music so as to make ends meet. I hope to be excused for the liberty I take in sending this letter. I only do it for the sake of charity and on account of hopes I entertain for the future of this little man.

His name then appeared in the role of College students of February 1892, being inscribed there as No. 51. When he arrived at the front door of

Manly College he was met by the President, Monsignor Verdon, with the words: "So you want to be a priest, young man" "I haven't made up my mind yet" was the reply. "Oh, you will after a while," said the Monsignor and accepted him.

After a couple of years, not yet having made up his mind to be a priest, Patrick left Manly for St Patrick's College, Goulburn, where he studied under Dr John Gallagher, classical scholar and later Bishop of Goulburn. The young man returned to Manly in 1898—this time to stay.

During the years at Manly young Patrick Hartigan was an avid reader of *The Bulletin*—surreptiously, of course, as it was very far from approved seminary fare. Writing under the pen-name of 'Mary Ann' he submitted a poem about an old race horse. One verse read:

> Ah, hang the saddle, the bridle and whip
> Let the cobwebs around them be spun
> No more with the sweat of old Trojan they'll drip
> For the horse and his rider are done.

The final verse was:

> Then bury me 'neath the shade of the box
> Where the magpies will welcome the morn
> Place a cross on my grave to show I expect
> A land where no protests annoy
> Where cheating ne'er harms the Almighty's elect
> Nor bitterness adds to their joy.

He was unwise enough to tell his friends of the pen-name he had used. Some weeks later the 'Red Page' of *The Bulletin* had the following:

> MARY ANN. The blanky bush person has been killed in these columns in all manners of ways, by horses falling on him, calves kicking him in the stomach and by an overdose of religion and everything from dead wattle boughs to bad poetry has been strewn on his tomb. See if you can kill him in a new way and add something fresh.

It did not take long for the whole student body to hear of the fate of 'Mary Ann' and many months were to pass before they allowed the budding poet to forget it. Patrick Hartigan did not abandon 'Mary Ann' and used the name for many years for contributions to *The Bulletin* and the *Albury Daily News*. Nor did he lose his respect for *The Bulletin*'s 'Red Page'—one of the gems he often quoted was:

> ANON. Your Poem: 'Lay in my arms, my darling' was obviously addressed to a hen.

Patrick Hartigan was ordained a priest at Sts Peter and Paul's Cathedral, Goulburn, on 18 January 1903 by his former teacher and life-long friend, Bishop John Gallagher. Albury was his first appointment where he was to spend seven years. As well as the ordinary duties of a priest in a country parish he took special interest in the young people and formed a Young Men's Society.

*Father Patrick Hartigan's ('John O'Brien's') parents, Patrick (aged sixty-six) and Mary (aged sixty-two), photographed in 1908.*

Above: *Seven of the nine Hartigan children photographed about 1888: from left, Mary Ellen (aged seven), Jane (aged eleven), Lily (aged fifteen), Annie (aged five), Bridgid (aged thirteen), Michael (aged three) and Patrick (nearly ten).*

Far right: *Father Patrick Hartigan ('John O'Brien'), aged about fifteen.*

Right: *Two of the Hartigan girls photographed about 1890: left, Bridgid (later Sister Ignatius) aged about fourteen, and Jane (later Sister Michael) aged about twelve.*

CREELMAN                    SYDNEY

He tells us the story of one of the young people there:

> Many years ago when I was a self-confident young curate in the first parish to which I was appointed, there was a little boy at the convent school who used to be brought out to sing and recite for the entertainment of visitors. He rose to something like fame among his small contemporaries who called him 'The Joker' and predicted a big career for him. It was then I came into the picture. I 'trained' him for the local Eisteddfod. Machinely crammed with ten verses or so of a hard luck story he faced the adjudicator and lost hopelessly, but fairly. Unknown to me, and uncoached by me, he had entered himself for other sections at the same competitions—all of which he won.

'The Joker' was later to become very successful at reciting 'John O'Brien's' verse and was in demand all over Australia. The poet-priest paid him this gracious tribute:

> He brings to the interpretation of these a sentiment —both Australian and Irish—which renders him singularly suitable for the work. I have heard him 'do' them many times, and must confess that he makes them appear new and fresh—even to me, their perpetrator.

It was at this time that he wrote in the *Australasian Catholic Record*: 'A Plea for Australian Literature'. While others were berating this country for its poor efforts in literature 'John O'Brien' gave credit for what had been done despite the difficulties associated with settlement in a new land.

He saw a sad note running through the works of such early writers as Henry Kendall, Adam Lindsay Gordon and Marcus Clarke; this is not surprising if our convict beginnings are taken into consideration. W.H. Ogilvie, 'Banjo' Paterson and Henry Lawson he lauded as presenting a brighter and truer picture, and he himself was to write with gladness and hope. He made this plea:

> We must recognise our literature in order that we may recognise our own land. We have a good country here, despite the hard things homesick exiles are continually saying about it. If it does not become great it is because we are half-hearted patriots mouthing empty nothings on every platform about a 'rising nation' and 'a glorious destiny' while at the same time we are pining after old world customs and old world traditions, and in our heart of hearts we wish we were not Australians.

During his time at Albury he first manifested his sympathy and understanding for those of other faiths. He was an ecumenist before it was fashionable, and he combined this with a firm faith in his own Church which he always loved dearly and served well.

In 1910 he was made Inspector of Catholic Schools of the diocese of Goulburn, New South Wales, and went to live at Thurgoona on the outskirts of Albury. He had an immense area to cover—from Goulburn to the east to Tocumwal and Narrandera on the west, the Lachlan River to the north, the Murray River and the Australian Alps to the south. He enjoyed the work and showed himself a sympathetic and competent examiner.

Early in 1911 he invested in a car, a second-hand eight horsepower Renault, which he bought in Sydney. He had to learn to drive it there and was terrified. He tried to honk everything out of his way, even the trams.

With the Renault he did an epic sick call to Bringenbong on the Upper Murray River. The sick man, named Riley, turned out to be none other than 'The Man from Snowy River' immortalised by 'Banjo' Paterson.

*Father Patrick Hartigan ('John O'Brien') photographed in 1910, aged about thirty-two.*

Left: *The poet and a passenger outside the Orphanage, Thurgoona, via Albury, about 1911. The car was an eight horsepower Renault.*

*Anne ('Annie') Hartigan (later Mecham) photographed shortly before her marriage in 1913.*

In the year 1916 Father Hartigan became parish priest of Berrigan, which also included Tocumwal further west on the Murray. He continued his writing and two of his poems are associated with this parish. Father Paddy Moloney, giving a mission there, told a beautiful story of his family in the country getting to Mass on Sundays. Father Hartigan's comment was: "I would have given a 'tenner' for that story—now I've got it free." 'The Old Mass Shandrydan' appeared shortly afterwards in *The Catholic Press*. When it was published in *Around the Boree Log* Father Moloney received a copy inscribed on the fly-leaf: 'To the suggestator from the perpetrator.'

The other poem linked with Berrigan is 'The Parting Rosary'. It concerns Edward Powell, a Berrigan lad who was killed in August 1916. The poem tells the story of his farewell party when he was taken aside by his mother to recite the Rosary.

In March 1917 Father Hartigan began what was to be a twenty-seven year stint as parish priest of Narrandera, New South Wales. He identified himself very much with that Riverina township on the Murrumbidgee River and became the friend of men and women of all creeds and none.

It was while he was there that *Around the Boree Log* was published. Father Joe Cusack, then in charge of St Francis' Church, Albion Street, Surry Hills in Sydney, had collected a scrap-book of Father Hartigan's poems contributed to *The Bulletin*, *The Catholic Press* and other journals. George Robertson of Angus and Robertson was invited over to the presbytery at Surry Hills and there the curate, Father Eris O'Brien (afterwards Archbishop of Canberra and Goulburn), read him some of the poems.

Next day George Robertson wrote to Father Hartigan:

They are the best we have come across since the

'Sentimental Bloke' happened along, and we want to publish them. The tenderness and humour of the verses have made of me a friend for a life.

Robertson went on to say:

I was telling one of my partners about my 'find' this morning, and he said, "Get him to immortalise Father Phelan of St Marys (near Penrith)." He used to steal his own fowls and take them to the sick—Catholic or Protestant it made no difference to him—with apologies for the feathers as his house-keeper 'had no time to pluck them'.

His Reverence's indifference to the loss of pair after pair (they always disappeared in pairs) made his housekeeper storm and, finally, invoke the local policeman's aid. Alas, the officer was probably an accessory both before and after the fact, and nothing came of that, so 'Josephine' lay in wait herself. Picture to yourself poor Father Phelan caught in the act of removing, in the dead of night, a couple of slabs from the wall of his own hen house!

Now isn't that a beautiful story? And it is true, too, for my partner says that a pair once came his way when he was a boy, and sick.

The book was published in September. The pen name 'John O'Brien' came from a milkman about whom the report was that water was added to his wares making a poor product and Father Hartigan had no pretensions that his jingles were any better.

*Around the Boree Log* was an instant success, the first edition of five thousand being sold almost immediately. The reviews were enthusiastic. C.J. Dennis in *The Bulletin* had this to say:

They are Australian first—bush Australian—they are Irish-Australian of course—but they are pure Australian too; good mates, good workers, full of healthy humour and a capacity for enjoyment that most of the world just now seems to have lost.

*Three of the Hartigan sisters photographed in 1925; from left, Mary Ellen (Sister Peter) aged about forty-four, Lily (Sister Gonzaga) aged about fifty-two, and Bridgid (Sister Ignatius) aged about fifty.*

The continued success of the *Boree Log* has proved George Robertson a prophet. With sales of over a quarter of a million copies it is in the same bracket as *The Sentimental Bloke* as a best seller in Australian poetry.

Father Hartigan remained in his beloved Narrandera until 1944 when advancing years and the desire to devote himself to historical writing caused his semi-retirement to the chaplaincy of the Convent of the Sacred Heart, Rose Bay. In the years 1943, 1944 and 1945 he produced in *The Australasian Catholic Record* a series of articles with the Latin title *In Diebus Illis*. These told the story of the pioneer priests—mostly Irish—who opened up the back country of Australia. These articles were later gathered into a book *The Men of '38* (Lowden, Kilmore, 1975).

It was during his years at Rose Bay that he wrote *On Darlinghurst Hill*, the history of the Sacred Heart parish there. It was marked by superb pen-pictures of the characters portrayed—Governor Darling's being a striking example.

Father Hartigan died in Lewisham Hospital on 27 December 1952 after an illness of a few months and his close friend Monsignor (now Cardinal) James Freeman wrote these memorable words in *The Catholic Weekly*:

When the last signs of serious illness started to make their sudden and ominous appearance, he was intrigued by the mystery, but as usual he kept his concern to himself. Solicitous enquirers were greeted with the same droll whimsicality which betrayed so little while it hid so much. Then as apparent recovery was followed by further attack in stern regularity it was obvious to his friends that there was something seriously wrong, but to no one was it more obvious than himself. What were his real thoughts during that period no one will ever know. Finally when he was told with gentle discretion that his illness could only have one end, that in fact, his days were numbered, he looked at death with the same calm detachment with which he always looked at life. "When a man has passed seventy," he said, "he has had a good innings and he shouldn't complain. At best, he could only have a few years more." So, propped up on his pillows with his strength failing every day, he waited for the end, serene and undisturbed, without any touch of melancholy or regret—watching the lights go out one by one and having no fear of the darkness because of the strong faith that burned brightly in his soul. Never was his life so grand as in the days of its passing.

He is buried with his parents at North Rocks cemetery—originally the burial ground for the Sisters of Mercy of Parramatta. Two of his sisters of that Congregation are buried there, as are Annie, her husband and their three invalid daughters, Jean, Cecily and Nance, for whom he felt so deeply.

Before his death Father Hartigan decided to have his unpublished poems gathered into a second collection for which he suggested the title *The Parish of St Mel's*. It was my task to edit them and they were published by Angus and Robertson in 1954.

One of them, 'The Durkins', is attributed to Dame Enid Lyons, widow of Joseph Lyons, Australia's fourteenth Prime Minister, who came up with the first line of a poem and could get no further. It ran: 'Have you ever seen the Durkins at the early morning Mass...' She went on to tell the story of this Devonport family notable for its involvement in the parish. Father Hartigan marshalled her ideas into a poem that is marked by a fine feeling for sound:

Yes, the altar-boy's a Durkin, proper, pious and
   sedate,
  And the choir is mostly Durkin kith and kin,
While a sober-sided Durkin, faith, he takes
   around the plate,
  And it's Durkin, Durkin, Durkin putting in.

*The Parish of St Mel's* is 'John O'Brien's' tribute to his beloved parish of Narrandera, and many of the verses in the book were written there.

The present illustrated edition is made up of selection from both *Around the Boree Log* and *The Parish of St Mel's*. The task of selection has been a difficult one in attempting to include and illustrate the most popular and representative of the poems.

Apart from Father Hartigan's published works, there remain some beautiful addresses to be found in the files of country newspapers and a few short stories and poems in *Manly*—the publication of the Manly priests—and elsewhere. This material has been gathered for a full biography that is now in preparation.

Besides the dwindling number of those who were priviledged to know 'John O'Brien' there are the thousands who never met him but have rightly divined from his published writings the kindliness and true humanity, the deep faith and love that were his. It is hoped that this beautifully illustrated edition of his poems will revive those memories and make new friends and admirers of 'John O'Brien', on this centenary of his birth.

Father F.A. Mecham
(nephew of Father Patrick Hartigan)

# PATRICK CARROLL

Patrick Carroll has become established as one of Sydney's most respected artists. He has held six highly successful exhibitions and received over thirty awards and commendations for his paintings, many from some of Australia's most noted artists.

Patrick describes himself as an "experimental realist". He has a great love for the Australian landscape and spends much of his time exploring the countryside of Australia for new subject matter and a deeper understanding of the bush as inspiration for his paintings. He has also experimented with a variety of subjects including portraiture, still life, character studies and life painting.

His work has been hung in the Wynne Prize at the Art Gallery of New South Wales and he is represented in municipal and country collections. His paintings have also been acquired by private collectors throughout Australia, the U.S.A, England, Japan and New Zealand.

Patrick was born and educated in the New South Wales country area of Bathurst in October 1949 and attended St Patrick's School and St Stanislaus' College there where first he was to read and admire John O'Brien's evocative verse. His love of painting also dates back to his childhood when his mother taught him the basics of oil and watercolour technique and encouraged him to draw. He furthered his artistic education at the Bathurst Technical College and later spent several years with the Royal Art Society of New South Wales in Sydney. He is now a member of that society and of the Drummoyne Art Society and the Australian Guild of Realist Artists.

He acknowledges many influences in his work over the past ten years: among them the Australian impressionists Tom Roberts, Arthur Streeton, Charles Conder, Walter Withers and Frederick McCubbin. His painting has also been given direction by the experiments of the French Impressionists, Post Impressionists and Fauves in his search for different approaches to painting. Having found a technique which suits his style he refines and extends it as he continues to experiment.

Patrick's first interest in illustrating the work of John O'Brien came from a suggestion by Patricia Rainsford of the Rainsford Gallery in Sydney. She suggested a one man exhibition of paintings inspired by O'Brien's verse. After consultation with the publishers of O'Brien's work, Angus & Robertson, the idea of a book of poems and paintings, and an exhibition, was enthusiastically agreed upon.

Before starting work on the paintings Patrick wanted to research fully John O'Brien (the *nom de plume* of Father Patrick Hartigan) and his poems. It was Father F.A. Mecham, the poet's nephew, and acknowledged expert on the subject, who provided extensive information on the Hartigan family history and background to the verse. Patrick also arranged for a special viewing, at the National

Library in Canberra, of a silent movie of *Around the Boree Log* made in the 1920s.

He then moved to the area around Yass in southern New South Wales where the Hartigan family had lived. Many of the illustrations are based on subjects found in his explorations there. Back in Sydney there were hours to be spent researching the period and delving into collections of early photographs of colonial life in New South Wales.

With the groundwork behind him the challenge of analysing the poems and interpreting them on canvas began. Although human figures were to play an important part in the majority of the paintings, wherever possible the artist let the landscape dominate and made the figures harmonize in colour and tone. He wanted to make each illustration a separate and complete work but also establish a unified relationship, an overall mood, from one painting to another.

Patrick Carroll best describes the background to the paintings:

> I found that I could closely identify with almost all of John O'Brien's poems firstly because of my own family life but perhaps, more importantly, because of my father's stories of his childhood days.
>
> Dad and his family lived in a small bush home on a property near Mudgee. He was one of 'twelve little steps and stairs'. He shared many a 'boree log'; had a 'little Irish mother', who added her 'trimmin's' to the rosary. He travelled miles to Mass in a contraption that must have closely resembled the 'Shandrydan'; he knew the Careys (he called them O'Reilly!); he knew Hanrahan (or was it Kennedy?); he rode to an old bush school on horseback; his place of worship was a church upon a hill. Father Pat was his friend and all his neighbours assembled in the paddocks to celebrate St Patrick's Day.
>
> With the volatile mixture of O'Brien's verse and Dad's tales in my mind, I proceeded, cautious-

ly, to begin my first work 'Around the Boree Log'.

While wandering through the bush near Yass I found a deserted old hut and made some hasty sketches of the interior. These later served as the framework for the painting. I wanted to capture the warmth of the old dwelling and used the 'boree log' (or fire-place) to project the closeness of the small room, and that of the people in it. I tried to make the characters as much a part of the hut as the fire and the old slab walls—some chatting among themselves and others beckoning the reader and viewer to join them by the fireside and enjoy the proceeding works in the mood they were intended.

'Six Brown Boxer Hats', as the title suggests, demanded that the hats were prominent in the painting. I felt that the disgruntled attitude of their wearers was equally important. So, I grouped them in the foreground and let their stances indicate their mood while the 'Little Irish Mother' looked on approvingly, and threateningly, in the middleground.

I based the 'Little Irish Mother' on my own grandmother who at eighty-six still has a twinkle in her eye. I did not attempt a strict likeness but chose to create a character that could be any little Irish mother 'With her head bowed and grey', and 'in her tattered faded gown'.

'The Old Bush School', and 'The Presbyt'ry Dog', were both lucky finds. On my way to Yass I stopped for lunch at Berrima and, as I ate, was rereading the poems. After driving on for a short distance I noticed a dirt track on my left. I followed it for a mile or so and stumbled upon the old bush school ('with its hat about its ears'). On closer inspection of the old dwelling (which seemed a little tired of supporting the weight of the hat), I found a smaller version of the 'Presbyt'ry Dog', gnawing on a bone at the back. The school I sketched, the dog I photographed (the scoundrel tried to steal my sketchbook).

Old 'Darkie' became the central figure in 'Ownerless'. I painted this work mainly from memory and found that the verse dictated the subject matter right down to the 'cobweb around the loose stirrup'.

'The Church Upon the Hill' was composed from a number of sketches from different localities: the church I found at Scone, the road belongs to Sofala, the foliage to Bathurst, and the parishioners to me!

My father agreed to pose for 'Peter Nelson' ('lonely stooped old Peter Nelson'). I used one of my brother's old felt hats and pushed up the top, borrowed my cousin's violin, and then sketched Dad standing and sitting with the instrument. In order to make him look sufficiently stooped I painted the top of the figure in the sitting position and then completed it in the standing pose.

The whole family posed for 'Said Hanrahan' —however, many adjustments were necessary during the execution of the work!

'The Old Mass Shandrydan' is a poem that I felt needed three illustrations to give a complete picture. I first painted a portrait of the vehicle from an old cart I found near Gundaroo, which, with a few minor alterations, did the job. Next, I painted the great 'procession' to Mass, which I placed in a landscape from Kootingal. The final work where the author reflects on the old days completed the statement.

'Laughing Mary' was inspired by an early photograph of my wife's mother, while the surrounding bush was located near Yass.

In illustrating the poems from the later collection, *The Parish of St Mel's* (first published in 1954), I chose only those that I felt were closely aligned with the period in which *Around the Boree Log* (first published in 1921) was set. The final poem, 'The Pastor of St Mel's', seemed to me to be a reflection not only on the life of the Pastor but a personal reminiscence by the poet on his own life. It is also the poem which bridges both the earlier and later collections of verse. As this was also my final work, I decided to allow the twilight mood of the painting suggest the feelings of the author and myself as the day faded and the work neared completion.

It was a challenging and rewarding task and, I hope, a fitting tribute to the man whose verse was first published more than fifty years ago but still continues to inspire and delight me and, I know, readers of all ages.

# AROUND THE BOREE LOG

Oh, stick me in the old caboose this night of wind and rain,
And let the doves of fancy loose to bill and coo again.
I want to feel the pulse of love that warmed the blood like wine;
I want to see the smile above this kind old land of mine.

So come you by your parted ways that wind the wide world through,
And make a ring around the blaze the way we used to do;
The "fountain" on the sooted crane will sing the old, old song
Of common joys in homely vein forgotten, ah, too long.

*The years have turned the rusted key, and time is on the jog,*
*Yet spend another night with me around the boree\* log.*

Now someone driving through the rain will happen in, I bet;
So fill the fountain up again, and leave the table set.
For this was ours with pride to say—and all the world defy—
No stranger ever turned away, no neighbour passed us by.

Bedad, he'll have to stay the night; the rain is going to pour—
So make the rattling windows tight, and close the kitchen door,
And bring the old lopsided chair, the tattered cushion, too—
We'll make the stranger happy there, the way we used to do.

*The years have turned the rusted key, and time is on the jog,*
*Yet spend another night with me around the boree log.*

He'll fill his pipe, and good and well, and all aglow within
We'll hear the news he has to tell, the yarns he has to spin;
Yarns—yes, and super-yarns, forsooth, to set the eyes agog,
And freeze the blood of trusting youth around the boree log.

Then stir it up and make it burn; the poker's next to you;
Come, let us poke it all in turn, the way we used to do.
There's many a memory bright and fair will tingle at a name—
But leave unstirred the embers there we cannot fan to flame.

*For years have turned the rusted key, and time is on the jog;*
*Still, spend this fleeting night with me around the boree log.*

\* Boree (sometimes accented on the last syllable) is the aboriginal name for the Weeping Myall—the best firewood in Australia except Gidgee.

PATRICK CARROLL

# PETER NELSON'S FIDDLE

Do you ever dream you hear it, you who went the lonely track?
   Do you ever hear its simple melodies
Tossing round deserted beaches, with the flotsam and the wrack,
   When the moonlight sprinkles silver on the trees?

Do you hearken now, I wonder, when the birds have gone to rest,
   And the blotted book of day once more is shut?
When the saffron stains have faded, and the swans have vanished west,
   Does your heart remember Peter Nelson's hut?

Lonely, stooped old Peter Nelson, with his "most peculiar" ways,
   With the clean-cut face, and hair as white as snow!
Something lingering round the old man seemed to tell of better days,
   Seemed to hint of love and laughter long ago.

Kindly silence wrapped the bushland; every warring note was still;
   Soft heart-tremors stirred, and smiling eyes grew dim.
Weaving fancies went the fiddle; dreams prophetic made us thrill—
   From the grave the visions stretched their hands to him.

There was rapture in the stillness; there were voices in the night;
   Trooped the angels with a beat of velvet wings;
And the stars stood still and listened, and the moon's face, strangely
     white,
   Kissed the sleeping world to dreams of better things.

Joy was lit in every corner, love was smiling at our side,
   Golden glamour o'er the dawning days was cast;
Gaily, gaily sang the fiddle, while we marched with swinging stride
   Through the flowers that hid the failures of the past.

Do you ever dream you hear it? Does it bring the vision back,
   With the curlew, and the moonlight on the trees?
Do the wavelets ripple shoreward with the flotsam as the wrack,
   When a fiddle plays the simple melodies?

Lonely, bent old Peter Nelson with the quaint, uncommon ways,
   "Spruced and tidied" when the book of day was shut,
With the dim light in the window, and the friends of better days
   Summoned round him by the fiddle in the hut.

PATRICK CARROLL —                              "PETER NELSON'S FIDDLE"

# THE LITTLE IRISH MOTHER

Have you seen the tidy cottage in the straggling, dusty street,
   Where the roses swing their censers by the door?
Have you heard the happy prattle and the tramp of tiny feet
   As the sturdy youngsters romp around the floor?
Did you wonder why the wiree* comes to sing his sweetest song?
   Did the subtle charm of home upon you fall?
Did you puzzle why it haunted you the while you passed along?—
   There's a Little Irish Mother there; that's all.

When you watched the children toiling at their lessons in the school,
   Did you pick a winsome girleen from the rest,
With her wealth of curl a-cluster as she smiled upon the stool,
   In a simple Monday-morning neatness dressed?
Did you mark the manly bearing of a healthy-hearted boy
   As he stood erect his well-conned task to tell?
Did you revel in the freshness with a pulse of wholesome joy?—
   There's a Little Irish Mother there as well.

There's a Little Irish Mother that a lonely vigil keeps
   In the settler's hut where seldom stranger comes,
Watching by the home-made cradle where one more Australian sleeps
   While the breezes whisper weird things to the gums,
Where the settlers battle gamely, beaten down to rise again,
   And the brave bush wives the toil and silence share,
Where the nation is a-building in the hearts of splendid men—
   There's a Little Irish Mother always there.

There's a Little Irish Mother—and her head is bowed and gray,
   And she's lonesome when the evening shadows fall;
Near the fire she "do be thinkin'," all the "childer" are away,
   And their silent pictures watch her from the wall.
For the world has claimed them from her; they are men and women
     now,
   In their thinning hair the tell-tale silver gleams;
But she runs her fingers, dozing, o'er a tousled baby brow—
   It is "little Con" or "Bridgie" in her dreams.

There's a Little Irish Mother sleeping softly now at last
   Where the tangled grass is creeping all around;
And the shades of unsung heroes troop about her from the past
   While the moonlight scatters diamonds on the mound.
And a good Australian's toiling in the world of busy men
   Where the strife and sordid grinding cramp and kill;
But his eyes are sometimes misted, and his heart grows brave again—
   She's the Little Irish Mother to him still.

When at last the books are balanced in the settling-up to be,
   And our idols on the rubbish-heap are hurled,
Then the Judge shall call to honour—not the "stars," it seems to me,
   Who have posed behind the footlights of the world;
But the king shall doff his purple, and the queen lay by her crown,
   And the great ones of the earth shall stand aside
While a Little Irish Mother in her tattered, faded gown
   Shall receive the crown too long to her denied.

*Also known as the Chocolate Wiree (pronounced "wiry"): a very fine songster, called by ornithologists "Rufous-breasted Whistler."

PATRICK CARROLL —                    "THE LITTLE IRISH MOTHER"

# TEN LITTLE STEPS AND STAIRS

There were ten little Steps and Stairs.
  Round through the old bush home all day
  Romping about in the old bush way.
They were ten little wild March hares,
  Storming the kitchen in hungry lines,
  With their naked feet, doing mud designs,
  "All over the place like punkin vines."
There were ten little Steps and Stairs.

There were ten little Steps and Stairs.
  In their home-made frocks and their Sunday suits,
  Up through the church with their squeaky boots,
While the folk went astray in their prayers,
  They hustled along, all dressed and neat—
  Oh, they bustled a bit as they filled the seat;
  From the first to the last, the lot complete.
There were ten little Steps and Stairs.

There were ten little Steps and Stairs.
  But the years have shuffled them all about,
  Have worn them thin, and straightened them out
With the tramp of a hundred cares;
  Ay, and each grim scar has a tale to tell
  Of a knock and a blow and a hand that fell,
  And a break in the line, and a gap. Ah, well—
There *were* ten little Steps and Stairs.

PATRICK CARROLL—                                    TEN LITTLE STEPS AND STAIRS

# THE OLD BUSH SCHOOL

'Tis a queer, old battered landmark that belongs to other years;
With the dog-leg fence around it, and its hat about its ears,
And the cow-bell in the gum-tree, and the bucket on the stool,
There's a motley host of memories round that old bush school—

With its seedy desks and benches, where at least I left a name
Carved in agricultural letters—'twas my only bid for fame;
And the spider-haunted ceilings, and the rafters, firmly set,
Lined with darts of nibs and paper (doubtless sticking in them yet),
And the greasy slates and blackboards, where I oft was proved a fool
And a blur upon the scutcheon of the old bush school.

There I see the boots in order—"'lastic-sides" we used to wear—
With a pair of "everlastin's" cracked and dusty here and there;
And we marched with great "high action"—hands behind and eyes
    before—
While we murdered "Swanee River" as we tramped around the floor.

Still the scholars pass before me with their freckled features grave,
And a nickname fitting better than the name their mothers gave;
Tousled hair and vacant faces, and their garments every one
Shabby heirlooms in the family, handed down from sire to son.
Ay, and mine were patched in places, and half-masted, as a rule—
They were fashionable trousers at the old bush school.

There I trudged it from the Three-mile, like a patient, toiling brute,
With a stocking round my ankle, and my heart within my boot,
Morgan, Nell and Michael Joseph, Jim and Mary, Kate and Mart
Tramping down the sheep-track with me, little rebels at the heart;

Shivery grasses round about us nodding bonnets in the breeze,
Happy Jacks and Twelve Apostles* hurdle-racing up the trees,
Peewees calling from the gullies, living wonders in the pool—
Hard bare seats and drab gray humdrum at the old bush school.

Early rising in the half-light, when the morn came, bleak and chill;
For the little mother roused us ere the sun had topped the hill,
"Up, you children, late 'tis gettin'." Shook the house beneath her knock,
And she wasn't always truthful, and she tampered with the clock.

Keen she was about "the learnin'," and she told us o'er and o'er
Of our luck to have "the schoolin'" right against our very door.
And the lectures—Oh, those lectures to our stony hearts addressed!
"Don't be mixin' with the Regans and the Ryans and the rest"—

"Don't be pickin' up with Carey's little talkative kanats†"—
Well, she had us almost thinking we were born aristocrats.
But we found our level early—in disaster, as a rule—
For they knocked "the notions" sideways at the old bush school.

Down the road came Laughing Mary, and the beast that she bestrode
Was Maloney's sorry piebald she had found beside the road;
Straight we scrambled up behind her, and as many as could fit
Clung like circus riders bare-back without bridle-rein or bit,
On that corrugated backbone in a merry row we sat—
We propelled him with our school-bags; Mary steered him with her
    hat—
And we rolled the road behind us like a ribbon from the spool,
"Making butter," so we called it, to the old bush school.

What a girl was Mary Casey in the days of long ago!
She was queen among the scholars, or at least we thought her so;
She was first in every mischief and, when overwhelmed by fate,
She could make delightful drawings of the teacher on her slate.
There was rhythm in every movement, as she gaily passed along
With a rippling laugh that lilted like the music of a song;
So we called her "Laughing Mary," and a fitful fancy blessed
E'en the bashful little daisies that her dainty feet caressed.

PATRICK CARROLL                                    "THE OLD BUSH SCHOOL"

She had cheeks like native roses in the fullness of their bloom,
And she used to sing the sweetest as we marched around the room;
In her eyes there lurked the magic, maiden freshness of the morn,
In her hair the haunting colour I had seen upon the corn;
Round her danced the happy sunshine when she smiled upon the stool—
And I used to swap her dinners at the old bush school.

Hard the cobbled road of knowledge to the feet of him who plods
After fragile fragments fallen from the workshop of the gods;
Long the quest, and ever thieving pass the pedlars o'er the hill
With the treasures in their bundles, but to leave us questing still.
Mystic fires horizons redden, but each crimson flash in turn
Only lights the empty places in the bracken and the fern;
So in after years I've proved it, spite of pedant, crank, and fool,
Very much the way I found it at the old bush school.

The hawker with his tilted cart pulled up beside the fence,
And opened out his wondrous mart with startling eloquence;
All sorts of toys for girls and boys upon the grass he spread,
And dolls, dirt-cheap, that went to sleep when stood upon their head;
But our male hearts were beating high for balls and cricket-bats
When mother, with the business eye, bought six brown boxer hats.

Six out-of-date extinguishers that fitted us too soon—
Six ugly, upturned canisters—but through the afternoon
Our rage and scorn were overborne to see swift fingers flit
With pad and trim, around the rim, to make the stove-pipes fit.
So Monday morning came, and six "ungrateful young kanats"
Went off to school like lunatics in six brown boxer hats.

Then friends at every meeting showed an interest all too rare
Or chilled our faltered greetings with the silence of a stare;
And comrades who, we thought, were true indulged in vulgar jeers,
While willing fists of humorists slambanged them round our ears;
But worst of all the social smart from taunting plutocrats—
"Yez pinched them from the hawker's cart, them six brown boxer
    hats."

(Dress how we will, we feel it still, when friends will stop to chat,
To see a broad good-humoured smile is trained upon the hat.)
We could not fight with wonted might, for bitter black distress
Was in our souls, and on our polls the hateful ugliness.
We faced a fine barrage of sticks; and six "broke-up" kanats
Went home to meet the storm in six brown battered boxer hats.

*These names are often applied to the same bird; but Happy Jacks (*alias* Gray-crowned Babblers) are brown with white markings; Twelve Apostles (*alias* Apostle-Birds) are gray with brown wings. Peewees, in the next line, are of course Magpie Larks.

†The essential kanat (possibly a corruption of gnat) is undersized, mischievous, useless and perky.

PATRICK CARROLL — "SIX BROWN BOXER HATS" —

# WHEN THE CIRCUS CAME TO TOWN

When the circus came to town
With its coaches and four, and its steeds galore,
  And a band and a painted clown,
Out to the road with a shout we'd fly
To gape at the elephants trudging by,
And our hearts beat fast and our hopes ran high,
  As we followed it up and down;
For nought in the air, the sea, or sky
Could fill a spot in our youthful eye,
  When the circus came to town.

So after the show we went,
And we got in the way of the men when they
  Were rigging the circus tent,
And we knew that we stood on holy ground,
As we followed an empty van around—
And got for ourselves a belting sound,
  Which a charm to the business lent.
But we wagged it from school behind the pound,
Till some Jack Pudding our shelter found
  And word to headquarters sent.

When the circus came to town,
We swallowed hot tea with tears of glee,
  And rushed in a tumult down;
We took quite the full of our shilling's worth,
And roared at the dummy's ponderous girth,
Or yelled in a salvo of noisy mirth
  At the tricks of the painted clown.
Oh, wondrous thoughts in our minds had birth,
And we felt that the band was the best on earth,
  When the circus came to town.

We fondly recalled the scene,
Horses that pranced, and eyes entranced,
  And the smell of the kerosene;
The mule, and the monkey, and tall giraffe,
The "juggerlin'-man" with his magic staff,
The girl who went round with her photograph
  (And oh, but we thought her a queen!)
We started a show on our own behalf,
"Performed" on the back of a poddy calf,
  And sighed for the might-have-been.

Now the circus comes to town,
And it rattles along, and a bare-foot throng
  Is pacing it up and down;
And the elephants trudge as they trudged of yore,
With the shabby shebangs, and the steeds galore;
But the glee of the youngsters who shout and roar
  At the tricks of the painted clown
Is balm to my soul, and I call *encore*
To the forwsy old jokes I've heard before,
  When the circus came to town.

"THE KOOKABURRAS"                    PATRICK CARROLL

# THE KOOKABURRAS

Fall the shadows on the gullies, fades the purple from the mountain;
And the day that's passing outwards down the stairways of the sky,
With its kindly deeds and sordid on its folded page recorded,
Waves a friendly hand across the range to bid the world "good-bye."
Comes a buoyant peal of laughter from the tall, white, slender timber,
Rugged mirth that floods the bushland with the joy of brotherhood,
With the rustic notes sonorous of a happy laughing chorus,
When the kookaburras bless the world because the world is good.

Oh, 'tis good and clean and wholesome when we take the sheep-track
    homewards,
And the kindly kitchen chimney flaps its homely bannerets;
All our twigs of effort, shooting golden promise for the fruiting,
Bring a night in peace enfolded that a useful day begets.
Hopeful dreams, their visions weaving, steel our hearts against to-
    morrow,
And we dare the challenge, strengthened by today's assaults withstood;
Beam the pregnant days before us; and another laughing chorus
Wraps the world in rippling revelry, because the world is good.

Loving eyes to watch our coming, loving arms to twine around us—
Tender tendrils, soft and silken, firmer far than iron stay—
All our little world upholding, gentle hearts and home enfolding,
And a cheery, friendly neighbour dropping in upon his way:
Mellow joy the soul refreshes with the scented breath of heaven,
With the whispered songs of other spheres, hereafter understood:
Angels keep their sure watch o'er us: and another laughing chorus
Flings a vesper blessing round the world, because the world is good.

Ah, the memories that find me now my hair is turning gray,
Drifting in like painted butterflies from paddocks far away;
Dripping dainty wings in fancy—and the pictures, fading fast,
Stand again in rose and purple in the album of the past.
There's the old slab dwelling dreaming by the wistful, watchful trees,
Where the coolabahs are listening to the stories of the breeze;
There's homely welcome beaming from its big, bright friendly eyes,
With The Sugarloaf behind it blackened in against the skies;
There's the same dear happy circle round the boree's cheery blaze
With a little Irish mother telling tales of other days.
She had one sweet, holy custom which I never can forget,
And a gentle benediction crowns her memory for it yet;
I can see that little mother still and hear her as she pleads,
"Now it's getting on to bed-time; all you childer get your beads."
There were no steel-bound conventions in that old slab dwelling free;
Only this—each night she lined us up to say the Rosary;
E'en the stranger there, who stayed the night upon his journey, knew
He must join the little circle, ay, and take his decade too.
I believe she darkly plotted, when a sinner hove in sight
Who was known to say no prayer at all, to make him stay the night.
Then we'd softly gather round her, and we'd speak in accents low,
And pray like Sainted Dominic so many years ago;
And the little Irish mother's face was radiant, for she knew
That "where two or three are gathered" He is gathered with them too.

O'er the paters and the aves how her reverent head would bend!
How she'd kiss the cross devoutly when she counted to the end!
And the visitor would rise at once, and brush his knees—and then
He'd look very, very foolish as he took the boards again.
She had other prayers to keep him. They were long, long prayers in truth;
And we used to call them "Trimmin's" in my disrespectful youth.
She would pray for kith and kin, and all the friends she'd ever known,
Yes, and everyone of us could boast a "trimmin'" all his own.
She would pray for all our little needs, and every shade of care
That might darken o'er The Sugarloaf, she'd meet it with a prayer.
She would pray for this one's "sore complaint," or that one's "hurted hand,"
Or that someone else might make a deal and get "that bit of land";
Or that Dad might sell the cattle well, and seasons good might rule,
So that little John, the weakly one, might go away to school.
There were trimmin's, too, that came and went; but ne'er she closed without
Adding one for something special "none of you must speak about."
Gentle was that little mother, and her wit would sparkle free,
But she'd murder him who looked around while at the Rosary:
And if perchance you lost your beads, disaster waited you,
For the only one she'd pardon was "himself"—because she knew
He was hopeless, and 'twas sinful what excuses he'd invent,

So she let him have his fingers, and he cracked them as he went,
And, bedad, he wasn't certain if he'd counted five or ten,
Yet he'd face the crisis bravely, and would start around again;
But she tallied all the decades, and she'd block him on the spot,
With a "Glory, Daddah, Glory!" and he'd "Glory" like a shot.
She would portion out the decades to the company at large;
But when she reached the trimmin's she would put herself in charge;
And it oft was cause for wonder how she never once forgot,
But could keep them in their order till she went right through the lot.
For that little Irish mother's prayers embraced the country wide;
If a neighbour met with trouble, or was taken ill, or died,
We could count upon a trimmin'—till, in fact, it got that way
That the Rosary was but trimmin's to the trimmin's we would say.
Then "himself" would start keownrawning*—for the public good, we
    thought—
"Sure you'll have us here till mornin'. Yerra, cut them trimmin's
    short!"
But she'd take him very gently, till he softened by degrees—
"Well, then, let us get it over. Come now, all hands to their knees."
So the little Irish mother kept her trimmin's to the last,
Ever growing as the shadows o'er the old selection passed;
And she lit our drab existence with her simple faith and love,
And I know the angels lingered near to bear her prayers above,
For her children trod the path she trod, nor did they later spurn

To impress her wholesome maxims on their children in their turn.
Ay, and every "sore complaint" came right, and every "hurted hand";
And we made a deal from time to time, and got "that bit of land";
And Dad did sell the cattle well; and little John, her pride,
Was he who said the Mass in black the morning that she died;
So her gentle spirit triumphed—for 'twas this, without a doubt,
Was the very special trimmin' that she kept so dark about.

But the years have crowded past us, and the fledglings all have flown,
And the nest beneath The Sugarloaf no longer is their own;
For a hand has written "*finis*" and the book is closed for good—
There's a stately red-tiled mansion where the old slab dwelling stood;
There the stranger has her "evenings," and the formal supper's spread,
But I wonder has she "trimmin's" now, or is the Rosary said?
Ah, those little Irish mothers passing from us one by one!
Who will write the noble story of the good that they have done?
All their children may be scattered, and their fortunes windwards
    hurled,
But the Trimmin's on the Rosary will bless them round the world.

*Grumbling, "grousing."

# THE CHURCH UPON THE HILL

A simple thing of knotted pine
  And corrugated tin;
But still, to those who read, a sign,
A fortress on the farthest line
  Against the march of sin.

Though rich man's gold was lacking quite,
  We built it strong and sure,
With willing hands and (Faith's delight)
The savings spared, the widow's mite,
  The shillings of the poor.

Nor could it fail to meet the eye
  And reverent thoughts instil,
As there above the township high,
And pointing always to the sky,
  It stood upon the hill.

And through our lives in wondrous ways
  Its holy purpose led
From limpid lisping cradle-days
To where the silent moonlight lays
  White hands upon the dead.

For when the Holy Morning strung
  Its beads upon the grass,
You'd see us driving—old and young—
The tall white graceful trees among,
  On every road to Mass.

It brought the brave young mother there,
  Surrounded by her brood,
To wrap their tiny hearts in prayer,
And teach them how to cast their care
  Upon the Holy Rood.

It watched the little bush girl grow,
  And kept her life from harm,
Till, spotless as the virgin snow
In wreath and veil, it saw her go
  Upon her husband's arm.

It blessed strong, trembling shoulders bent:
  Helped many a soul in thrall
To climb again the steep ascent,
And reft the grim entanglement
  That brought about the fall.

It soothed the gray old mother's pain,
  A-swaying while she told
Her rosary o'er and o'er again,
For griefs that rent her heart in twain—
  So new, and ah, so old!

(There's "that poor boy who went astray,"
  And lined her gentle brow;
There's "them that's wand'rin' fur away,"
And "them that's in their grave to-day"
  And "beck'nin'" to her now.)

Refuge it gave the weary heart,
  Beyond the sordid din
And conflict of the crowded mart,
One sweet, sequestered nook apart,
  Where all might enter in.

Though high and grand cathedrals shine,
  To my mind grander still
Is that wee church of knotted pine,
That rampart on the outer line
  That stood upon the hill.

PATRICK CARROLL —

# ST PATRICK'S DAY

'Tis the greatest splash of sunshine right through all my retrospection
   On the days when fairies brought me golden dreams without alloy,
When I gazed across the gum-trees round about the old selection
   To the big things far beyond them, with the yearning of a boy.

Drab the little world we lived in; like the sheep, in slow procession
   Down the track along the mountain, went the hours upon their way,
Bringing hopes and idle longings that could only find expression
   In the riot of our bounding hearts upon St Patrick's Day.

There were sports in Casey's paddock, and the neighbours would
     assemble
   On the flat below the homestead, where the timber fringed the creek;
With Australian skies above them, and Australian trees a-tremble
   And the colours of the autumn set in hat and hair and cheek.

Mighty things were done at Casey's; mighty bouts anticipated
   Made the Sunday church-door topic for a month ahead at least;
On the cheerless Sundays after, with misguided hope deflated,
   We explained away our failures as we waited for the priest.

So when morning Mass was over, it was trot and break and canter
   Helter-skelter down to Casey's, banging, pounding all the way,
And the greetings flung in Irish, and the flood of Celtic banter,
   And the hectic flush of racial pride upon St Patrick's Day.

Everywhere was emerald flashing from the buggies, traps, and jinkers,
   There was green in every garment, and a splash in every hat,
In the bows upon the cart-whips, in the ribbons on the winkers,
   In the wealth of woven carpet 'neath the gums on Casey's Flat.

There the new dress faced the critics, and the little beaded bonnet
   And the feather flowing freely like a sapling in a gale;
And "himself" inside his long black coat that bore a bulge upon it
   Where for twelve forgotten months its weight had hung upon the
     nail;

And the "splather" of a necktie only once a year paraded,
   And the scarf that came from Ireland, "ere a one of you were born,"
And the treasured bunch of shamrock—old and withered now, and
     faded,
   Blessed by every tear that stained it since the cruel parting morn.

Mighty things were done at Casey's. Men of solid reputation,
   Ringing bells and giving orders, kept the programme moving by;
And they made you sickly conscious of your humble situation
   When they glared upon your meanness with a cold official eye.

Every "maneen" with a broken voice and backers there beside him,
   And his socks outside his breeches, was a hero in his way;
Every nag around the country with a raw bush lad astride him
   Was a racehorse with an Irish name upon St Patrick's Day.

Oh, the cheering that betokened those I knew so well competing,
   With their long legs throwing slip-knots, and the look of men in
     pain—
Put me back into the reach-me-downs, and let me hear the greeting,
   Set me loose in Casey's paddock, where I'd be a boy again!

Yes, 'twas good to be a pilgrim in a world that held such wonders,
   Though eternal bad behaviour put me 'neath parental ban,
Though the staring, and the wandering, and a score of general blunders
   Got me gaoled behind the taffrail of the Old Mass Shandrydan.

"Yerra, Johnnie, stop that gawkin'." Is it—with the pulses pumping,
   And the little heart high-stepping to the music of the drum—
Is it "stop it," with a something in the young blood madly thumping
   With a foreword of the purpose of the pregnant years to come?

Mighty things were done at Casey's. Mighty impulse was behind them,
   'Twas the sacred spark enkindled that was burning to the bone;
Never yet were men more loyal to the holy ties that bind them,
   And the love they gave their country made me conscious of my own.

Never yet were men more loyal. Be they met in thousands teeming,
  Be they gathered down at Casey's with their kindred and their kind;
They are marching on for Ireland, with the beauteous vision gleaming
  Of the altar-fires of Freedom in the land they left behind.

Not a torch was ever lighted at a tomb where Freedom slumbered,
  But it smouldered—grimly smouldered—till the stone was rolled
    away;
When it flashed across the half-light, rallying rocket glares unnumbered,
  Like the spangled blades of morning that bespeak the march of day.

Not a voice was ever lifted, but an echo never dying
  Flung the slogan once repeated when the hand was on the gun;
Though the prophet tongue was ashes, came the conquering banners
    flying
  With a dazzling watchword flashing, blazing signals in the sun.

Yes, the world has ever seen it in its journey down the ages,
  Seen it writ in living scarlet in the blood that has been shed;
And a hand re-writes the head-line deep across the lurid pages,
  When the stricken, fearless living meet the deathless, martyred dead.

Thrills a leaping thought within me, when I see a land around me
  That has never seen the foeman's steel, nor heard the foeman's shot,
At whose shrine I lit the tapers, when her witching sweetness bound me
  With an iron vow of service of a pulsing pride begot;

To that big free land I've given all the love that courses through me;
  That her hands have rocked my cradle stirs my heart in every beat.
An Australian, ay, Australian—oh, the word is music to me,
  And the craven who'd deny her would I spurn beneath my feet.

Thrills the thought that, did the traitor stretch a tainted hand to foil her,
  Did I see her flag of silver stars a tattered thing and torn,
Did I see her trampled, breathless, 'neath the shod heel of the spoiler,
  And her bleeding wounds a byword, and her name a thing of scorn,

There would flash the living bayonets in the strong hands of my bro-
    thers,
  And the blood that coursed for nationhood, through all the years of
    pain,
In the veins of patriot fathers and of Little Irish Mothers
  Would be hot as hissing lava streams to thrill the world again.

# SAID HANRAHAN

"We'll all be rooned," said Hanrahan,
  In accents most forlorn,
Outside the church, ere Mass began,
  One frosty Sunday morn.

The congregation stood about,
  Coat-collars to the ears,
And talked of stock, and crops, and drought,
  As it had done for years.

"It's lookin' crook," said Daniel Croke;
  "Bedad, it's cruke, me lad,
For never since the banks went broke
  Has seasons been so bad."

"It's dry, all right," said young O'Neil,
  With which astute remark
He squatted down upon his heel
  And chewed a piece of bark.

And so around the chorus ran
  "It's keepin' dry, no doubt."
"We'll all be rooned," said Hanrahan,
  "Before the year is out.

"The crops are done; ye'll have your work
  To save one bag of grain;
From here way out to Back-o'-Bourke
  They're singin' out for rain.

"They're singin' out for rain," he said,
  "And all the tanks are dry."
The congregation scratched its head,
  And gazed around the sky.

"There won't be grass, in any case,
  Enough to feed an ass;
There's not a blade on Casey's place
  As I came down to Mass."

"If rain don't come this month," said Dan,
  And cleared his throat to speak—
"We'll all be rooned," said Hanrahan,
  "If rain don't come this week."

A heavy silence seemed to steal
  On all at this remark;
And each man squatted on his heel,
  And chewed a piece of bark.

"We want a inch of rain, we do,"
  O'Neil observed at last;
But Croke "maintained" we wanted two
  To put the danger past.

"If we don't get three inches, man,
  Or four to break this drought,
We'll all be rooned," said Hanrahan,
  "Before the year is out."

In God's good time down came the rain;
  And all the afternoon
On iron roof and window-pane
  It drummed a homely tune.

And through the night it pattered still,
  And lightsome, gladsome elves
On dripping spout and window-sill
  Kept talking to themselves.

It pelted, pelted all day long,
  A-singing at its work,
Till every heart took up the song
  Way out to Back-o'-Bourke.

And every creek a banker ran,
  And dams filled overtop;
"We'll all be rooned," said Hanrahan,
  "If this rain doesn't stop."

And stop it did, in God's good time;
  And spring came in to fold
A mantle o'er the hills sublime
  Of green and pink and gold.

And days went by on dancing feet,
  With harvest-hopes immense,
And laughing eyes beheld the wheat
  Nid-nodding o'er the fence.

And, oh, the smiles on every face,
  As happy lad and lass
Through grass knee-deep on Casey's place
  Went riding down to Mass.

While round the church in clothes genteel
  Discoursed the men of mark,
And each man squatted on his heel,
  And chewed his piece of bark.

"There'll be bush-fires for sure, me man,
  There will, without a doubt;
We'll all be rooned," said Hanrahan,
  "Before the year is out."

PATRICK CARROLL —                                    "SHILLAILHANAN"

# THE ALTAR-BOY

Now McEvoy was altar-boy
  As long as I remember;
He was, bedad, a crabbed lad,
  And sixty come December.
Faith, no one dared to "interfare"
  In things the which concernin'
'Twas right and just to him to trust
  Who had the bit o' learnin'
To serve the priest; and here at least
  He never proved defaulter;
So, wet or dry, you could rely
  To find him on the Altar.

The acolyte in surplice white
  Some admiration rouses:
But McEvoy was altar-boy
  In "Sund'y coat-'n-trouses."
And out he'd steer, the eye severe
  The depths behind him plumbin',
In dread, I wot (he once was "cot"),
  The priest might not be comin':
Then, stepping slow on heel and toe,
  No more he'd fail or falter,
But set likewise with hands and eyes
  He'd move about the Altar.

A master-stroke of other folk
  Might start the opposition,
And some, mebbe, in jealousy
  Bedoubt their erudition;
But McEvoy was altar-boy
  And, spite of all their chattin',
It "put the stuns" on lesser ones
  To hear him run the Latin.
And faith, he knew the business through,
  The rubrics and the psalter;
You never met his "aikals" yet
  When servin' on the Altar.

The priest, indeed, might take the lead
  By right of Holy Orders,
But McEvoy was altar-boy,
  And just upon the borders.
So sermons dry he'd signify
  With puckered brows behoovin',
An', if you please, at homilies
  He'd nod the head approvin';
And all the while a cute old smile
  Picked out the chief defaulter;
Faith, wet or dry, the crabbéd eye
  Would "vet" you from the Altar.

# AT CASEY'S AFTER MASS

There's a weather-beaten sign-post where the track turns towards the
  west,
Through the tall, white, slender timber, in the land I love the best.
Short its message is—"To Casey's"—for it points the road to Casey's;
And my homing heart goes bushwards on an idle roving quest,
Down the old, old road contented, o'er the gum-leaves crisp and scented,
Where a deft hand splashed the purple on the big hill's sombre crest.
Ah, it's long, long years and dreary, many, many steps and weary,
Back to where the lingering dew of morn bedecked the barley-grass,
When I watched the wild careering of the neighbours through the
  clearing
Down that sweet bush track to Casey's, o'er the paddock down to
  Casey's;
Spending Sunday down at Casey's after Mass.

For, as soon as Mass was over, round the church they swarmed like bees,
Filled their pipes and duly lit them, brushed the dust from off their
  knees;
Then they'd "ready-up" for Casey's—self-invited down to Casey's—
Harness horses for the women with a bushman's careless ease.
With a neat spring to the saddle, soon would start the wild skedaddle,
Passing gigs and traps and buggies packed as tight as they could squeeze;
Hearts as buoyant as a feather in the mellow autumn weather,
While the noisy minahs cheered to see the glad procession pass—
All the Regans and the Ryans, and the whole mob of O'Briens
Bringing up the rear to Casey's—in the Shandrydan to Casey's—
Spending Sunday down at Casey's after Mass.

Past the kitchen door they rattled and they took the horses out;
While the women went inside at once, the men-folk hung about
Round the stable down at Casey's, waiting dinner down at Casey's;
And they talked about the Government, and blamed it for the drought,
Sitting where the sunlight lingers, picking splinters from their fingers,
Settling all the problems of the world beyond a chance of doubt.
From inside there came the bustle of the cheerful wholesome hustle,
As dear old Mrs Casey tried all records to surpass;
Oh, there's many a memory blesses her sweet silver-braided tresses;

They were "lovely" down at Casey's—always joking down at
  Casey's—
Spending Sunday down at Casey's after Mass.

So they called us in to dinner, five-and-twenty guests—and more—
At the longest kitchen-table ever stood upon a floor.
There was plenty down at Casey's—ay, an open house was Casey's,
Where the neighbour and his missus never, never passed the door;
Where they counted kindly giving half the joy and pride of living
And the seasons came full-handed, and the angels blessed the store;
While the happy Laughing Mary flitted round us like a fairy.
And the big, shy boys stopped business, and looked up to watch her
  pass—
Ah, but when she caught them staring at the ribbons she was wearing!
Well, they spilled their tea at Casey's—on the good clean cloth at
  Casey's—
Spending Sunday down at Casey's after Mass.

Then the reckless feats of daring, and the bushman's fierce delight
When the brumby squealed and rooted, and the saddle-girths were
  tight!
They could ride 'em down at Casey's—stick like plasters down at
  Casey's—
When they noticed Mary looking, they would go with all their might;
Ho! they belted, and they clouted, and they yelled, and whooped, and
  shouted,
"Riding flash" to "ketch" the ladies, spurring, flogging, left and right!
And the lad with manners airy risked his neck for Laughing Mary
When he summoned all his courage up a rival to surpass;
Oh, the fun went fast and faster, as he landed in disaster
In the puddle-hole at Casey's—with his brand new suit at Casey's—
Spending Sunday down at Casey's after Mass.

Hoary, hale bewhiskered veterans, perched like mopokes in a row,
Out of danger on the top-rail, gave advice to those below;
They were wonders down at Casey's, were the old men at the Caseys'—
They're the boys could ride the "bad 'uns" in the days of long ago!

Faith, and old man Casey told 'em of a way he had to hold 'em.
Man, "the deuce an outlaw thrun him," when he "got a proper show";
Ay, and each man "upped and showed 'em" how he "handled 'em,
    an' rode 'em"—
Pshaw! there never was a native these old riders could outclass.
Once again they were "among 'em," and they "roped 'em" and they
    "slung 'em"
On the stockyard fence at Casey's—smoking, "pitchin'," down at
    Casey's—
Spending Sunday down at Casey's after Mass.

Hard and cold is youth to fancies which around the old men cling;
So they left them perched upon the rail to swap their vapouring,
Took a seat inside at Casey's, on the good chairs at the Caseys';
While the Caseys' new piano made the old house rock and ring.
There their mild eyes stared and glistened, as they sat around and
    listened
To the tuneful little ditties Laughing Mary used to sing;
There they rubbed their chins and reckoned that to no one was she
    second—
"Cripes, she'd sing the blooming head off any singer in her class!"
And the banter and the laughter when the chorus hit the rafter!
It was "great" to be at Casey's—healthy, wholesome fun at Casey's—
Spending Sunday down at Casey's after Mass.

There was something in the old life which I cannot quite forget;
There are happy golden memories that hover round me yet—
Something special down at Casey's, in that wonderland of Casey's,
Where the crowfoot and the clover spread a dowry coverlet,
Where the trees seemed always greener, where the life of man was
    cleaner,
And the joys that grew around us shed no leaves of brown regret.
Oh, the merry, merry party! oh, the simple folk and hearty,
Who can fling their cares behind them, and forget them while they pass
Simple lives and simple pleasure never stinted in the measure.

There was something down at Casey's, something clean and good at
    Casey's—
Spending Sunday down at Casey's after Mass.

Passed and gone that old bush homestead where the hours too swiftly
    flew;
Silent now the merry voices of the happy friends I knew;
We have drifted far from Casey's. All deserted now is Casey's—
Just a lone brick chimney standing, and a garden-tree or two.
Still the minahs love to linger where the sign-post points the finger
Down the bush track winding westward where the tall white timber
    grew.
But the big hill seems to wonder why the ties are snapped asunder,
Why the neighbours never gather, never loiter as they pass;
Yet a tear-stained thought beseeming comes along and sets me dreaming
That I'm back again at Casey's, with the old, old friends at Casey's;
Spending Sunday down at Casey's after Mass.

PATRICK CARROLL                             "AT CASEY'S AFTER MASS"

# TEDDO WELLS, DECEASED

Times I think I'm not the man—
  Must be some mistake.
Me among the also ran?
  Cute and wideawake!
Old and beat and crotchety—
  Sixty-five, at least—
Knockin' round the presbytery,
  Groomin' for the priest,
Choppin' wood, and ringin' bells,
Dodgin' work and takin' spells!
Me all right, one Ed'ard Wells
  (Late Teddo Wells, deceased)—
Wheelin' barrows round the yard,
Gammon to be workin' hard,
  A-groomin' for the priest!

Trainin' prads was Teddo's game;
  Made a tidy bit.
Everybody knew the name,
  Teddo Wells was "It."
Bought that bit of property
  (Value since increased),
Gettin' on tremendously,
  Married by the priest.
Papers full of Teddo Wells,
Trainin' horses for the swells;
Since redooced to ringin' bells
  (Teddo Wells, deceased)
Shinin' boots and learnin' sense,
Nailin' palin's on the fence,
  A-groomin' for the priest.

Lost that bit of property,
  Ended up in smoke—
Too much "Jimmie Hennessy"—
  Down, and stony-broke.
Used to think he knew the game
  Till they had him fleeced.
"Mud" is this 'ere hero's name,
  Workin' for the priest—
Unbeknown to sports and swells;
They've no time for Ed'ard Wells.
Up the spout and ringin' bells
  As "Teddo Wells, deceased";
Never noticed up the town,
Never asked to keep one down—
  Groomin' for the priest.

Times I stops a cove to chat,
  One as gamed and spieled;
Chips me in the curate's hat,
  "Six to four the field."
"What-o! Teddo Wells," sez he,
  "Him that horses leased,
Owned that bit of property,
  Groomin' for the priest?"
"Guessin' eggs and seen the shells;
Brains," sez I, "and breedin' tells,
This old gent is Ed'ard Wells,
  Late Teddo Wells, deceased.
Ringin' bells is Ed'ard's game,
Openin' doors and closin' same,
  Called 'groomin'' for the priest.'"

Never see a horse nohow,
  Just an old machine;
Always in a tearin' row
  With this Josephine.
Got an eye that makes you feel
  Well and truly p'liced,
Follerin' out upon your heels,
  A-goin' to tell the priest.
"Can't smoke here now, Ed'ard Wells,
That old pipe offensive smells;
Go and smoke outside," she yells.
  So Teddo Wells, deceased,
Him that once was in the boom,
Wood-heap has for smokin' room—
  A-groomin' for the priest.

Times I says it's all a joke
  Someone's puttin' up;
Me dead-beat and stony-broke,
  Me that won a cup,
Owned that bit of property,
  Them good horses leased!
Kickin' round the presbytery
  A-groomin' for the priest!
Choppin' wood and ringin' bells,
Curby-hocked and takin' spells!
Me it is, one Ed'ard Wells,
  (Late Teddo Wells, deceased)
Smokin' hard and talkin' free
Of the man he used to be,
  And groomin' for the priest.

# CALLING TO ME

Through the hush of my heart in the spell of its dreaming
  Comes the song of a bush boy glad-hearted and free;
Oh, the gullies are green where the sunlight is streaming,
  And the voice of that youngster is calling to me.

It is calling to me with a haunting insistence,
  And my feet wander off on a hoof-beaten track,
Till I hear the old magpies away in the distance
  With a song of the morning that's calling me back.

It is calling me back, for the dew's on the clover,
  And the colours are mellow on mountain and tree;
Oh, the gold has gone gray in the heart of the rover,
  And the bush in the sunshine is calling to me.

It is calling to me, though the breezes are telling
  Gay troubadour tales to the stars as they roam;
For the tapers are lit in the humble old dwelling,
  And the love that it sheltered is calling me home.

It is calling me home—but the white road lies gleaming,
  And afar from it all must I tarry and dree;
Just an echo far off, in the hush of my dreaming,
  Is the voice of a youngster that's calling to me.

Come, Little One, and sing to me
    A song our big wide land to bless,
Around whose gentle parent-knee
    We've twined the flowers of kindliness.

Your eyes are clear Australian blue,
    Your voice like soft bush breezes blown;
Her sunshine steeps the heart of you,
    Your tresses are the wattle's own.

What, no Australian song, my child,
    No lay of love, no hymn of praise?
And yet no mother ever smiled
    With our dear country's winsome ways:

You sing the songs of all the earth,
    Of bower and bloom and bird and bee;
And has the land that gave you birth
    No haunting, native melody?

Your poets' eager pens awake
    The world-old themes of love and youth,
The pulse of life, the joy, the ache,
    The pregnant line of earnest truth;

They dress you these in native guise,
    And interweave with loving hand
The freshness of your rain-washed skies,
    The colours of your sunlit land.

What, no Australian song, my dear?
    And yet I've heard the cottage ring
With notes the world would pause to hear,
    When at their work your sisters sing.

They sing the songs of all the earth,
    Of tender sky, and dimpling sea,
But all their strains have not the worth
    Of one Australian song, for me.

I've heard the harp the breezes play
    Among the wilding wilga-trees;
I've swept my world of care away
    When bush birds lift their melodies;

I've seen the paddocks all ablaze
    When spring in golden glory comes,
The purple hills of summer days,
    The autumn ochres through the gums;

I've seen the bright folk riding in
    O'er blooms that deck the clovered plain,
And 'neath the trees, when moonbeams spin
    Their silver-dappled counterpane.

What, no Australian song, my pet?
    No patriot note on native horn,
To bind the hearts in kindness met,
    And link the leal Australian-born?

Yet every exile, wandering lone
    Our happy careless homes among,
May live the best his heart has known
    Whene'er his country's songs are sung.

You sing the songs of all the earth,
    Of alien flower and alien tree:
But no one, in my grief or mirth,
    Will sing Australian songs to me.

You sing of every land but mine,
    Where life is lilting 'neath the sun.
Still all its spirit seems ashine
    In you, my little laughing one.

Your eyes are clear Australian blue,
    Your face is towards the future set:
The bounding, gladsome heart of you
    Is hers—and only hers, my pet.

Ah, Little One, what dreams would rise
    If, nestled here upon my knee,
You'd flash those soft Australian eyes,
    And sing your country's songs to me!

Patrick Carroll 1977

I can see it in my dreaming o'er a gap of thirty years,
And the rattle of its boxes still is music in my ears:
With a bow to family vanity it rises from the past
As the pride of the selection where my humble youth was cast.
It was fashioned in a nightmare by some wandering genius,
And it wasn't quite a waggon, and it wasn't quite a 'bus;
'Twas an old four-wheeled gazabo that was something in between,
And the wheels were painted yellow, and the rest was painted green
(It would waken lively interest in the antiquarian)
And 'twas known to all the country as the Old Mass Shandrydan.

It did duty on a week-day in a dozen ways and more,
And it seemed just made to order for whate'er 'twas wanted for;
It would cart the chaff to market, carry wood and hay in turn,
And the neighbours in rotation used to cadge the old concern.
But the Sundays we were due for Mass would cancel every loan,
For the Little Irish Mother then would claim it for her own.
She inspected it the day before (and criticized it, too),
And the ten of us were set to work to make it look like new.
There was one to every yellow wheel—ay, one to every spoke;
One to nail a piece of hardwood on the part "them Careys" broke:
Another from the floor of it the chips and straw would rake,
While the Dad went searching rubbish-heaps for old boots for the
      brake:
So we rubbed and scrubbed and hammered up, and beat the rattertan
Till it stood in all its glory as the Old Mass Shandrydan.

When at last, with velvet sandals shod, the Holy Morning crept
Through the mists above The Sugarloaf, that silent vigil kept
O'er a little old slab dwelling which the years have brushed away,
You would hear the Little Mother stirring round before the day,
Rousing sleepy heads from blankets, washing faces, doing hair,
Scolding, coaxing, bustling, breathless in her hurry everywhere.
Half the night before she laboured, and we'd hear her come and go
With the Sunday suits of "reach-me-downs" to place them in a row.
There was this to patch, and that to darn, and something else to mend;

PATRICK CARROLL —                                    THE OLD MASS SHANDRYDAN.

She would see to every single thing before her work would end,
To the dresses and the pinnies—oh, the memory she had!—
There were lace-up boots for Morgan, and a clean white shirt for Dad.
And the hubbub and the murder that the household used to make,
When she had us tumbled out of bed, and painfully awake.
Here a voice in anguish lifted to announce a button gone;
Someone calling from the back-room "Mum, what socks will I put on?"
While "himself" was like a Bolshevik athirst for human blood,
Shouting "Mother," as he wrastled with a fractious collar-stud.
But she kept the tumult under till she had us spick and span,
Packed like pickles in a bottle in the Old Mass Shandrydan.

We had ten good miles to drive to Mass—and Mass was sharp at eight;
But we'd never hear the end of it if something kept us late;
So we started ere the morning hung its bunting in the sky,
And the kookaburras chortled as we rumbled slowly by.
For the frost was on the barley, and the rime was on the trees,
And our little faces smarted with the whip-lash of the breeze,
Still we watched the branches redden to the first kiss of the sun
And we counted all the cart-wheels that the busy spiders spun,
Then the magpies sang to greet us, and our little hearts began
To forget that we were shivering in the Old Mass Shandrydan.

So the old contraption lumbered, safely towed, as Dad knew how,
By a pair of hefty elephants promoted from the plough
And it rattled like a saw-mill, and it thundered like a dray;
Faith, you'd hear the circus coming a half-a-dozen miles away!
All along the road the neighbours used to take the time from us,
For they never made a start until they heard our omnibus;
Then a shrill soprano shouted, "Put the horses in the van.
"Them's The Sugarloaf O'Briens in the Old Mass Shandrydan."

We were first to Carey's Crossing, first to reach Moloney's Mill,
But the opposition caught us as we laboured up the hill;
Then the air became electric as they tried to pass us by,
For "himself" for family reasons (which I needn't specify)
Kept the road in deadly earnest, and would never seem to hear
The abuse of the procession that was gathering in the rear.

PATRICK CARROLL — 1910 —                                          "THE OLD MAIL SHARPLEY DAM"

Oh, they whistled and they shouted till their feelings overflowed,
But the old man in the Dreadnought was the master of the road.
It was suicide to bump it, and the horses wouldn't shy,
So he trundled on before them with a bad look in his eye.
Then, as suddenly the whistling and the bantering shouting ceased
And a solemn hush denoted the arrival of the priest,
Would a fine "good Catholic" thunder "Yerra, shame upon you, man!
Pull one side there, Pat O'Brien, with your Old Mass Shandrydan."

Pull! Bedad, he'd pull the town down when His Reverence hove in
  sight,
Pulled his hat off with the left hand, and pipe out with the right;
Pulled his family in the gutter, pulled the horses off their feet,
And a shower of small O'Briens went skedadcling from the seat.
Then they rattled loudly past us, and a wild stampede began,
For they all had family reasons to outpace the other man.
There were buggies, traps, and turnouts there of every shape and rig;
There were Murphys in a spring-cart, and the Caseys in a gig;
There were Barnes' ponies pounding twixt a gallop and a trot,
While the Careys with their pacing-mare went sailing past the lot.
Faith, we had it in for Carey, and our disrespect increased
At the cheek of "them there Careys who would try to beat the priest."
No, we wouldn't stoop to things like that; we'd act the gentleman
Half a mile behind the others in the Old Mass Shandrydan.

It's a long way back I'm gazing, and the stage has changed since then;
Just an echo finds me sometimes, bringing back the scene again.
Oh, the heart beats slower measure than it used to beat, alas,
When a Little Irish Mother dressed us all in time for Mass.
I have lounged in fast expresses, I have travelled first saloon,
I have heard the haunting music that the winds and waters croon,
I have seen the road careering from a whirring motor-car,
Where the Careys couldn't pass us, or our sense of fitness jar;
But the world is somehow smaller, somehow less enchanting than
When I saw it o'er the tail-board of the Old Mass Shandrydan.

PATRICK CARROLL — "THE OLD PLACE SHATTERWYNN"

# THE PRESBYT'RY DOG

Now of all the old sinners in mischief immersed,
　From the ages of Gog and Magog,
At the top of the list, from the last to the first,
And by every good soul in the parish accursed,
　Is that scamp of a Presbyt'ry Dog.

He's a hairy old scoundrel as ugly as sin,
　He's a demon that travels incog.,
With a classical name, and an ignorant grin,
And a tail, by the way, that is scraggy and thin,
　And the rest of him merely a dog.

He is like a young waster of fortune possessed,
　As he rambles the town at a jog;
For he treats the whole world as a sort of a jest,
While the comp'ny he keeps—well, it must be confessed
　It's unfit for a Presbyt'ry Dog.

He is out on the street at the sound of a fight,
　With the eyes on him standing agog,
And the scut of a tail—well, bedad, it's a fright;
Faith, you'd give him a kick that would set him alight,
　But you can't with the Presbyt'ry Dog.

His rotundity now to absurdity runs,
　Like a blackfellow gone to the grog;
For the knowing old shaver the presbyt'ry shuns
When it's time for a meal, and goes off to the nuns,
　Who're deceived in the Presbyt'ry Dog.

When he follows the priest to the bush, there is war.
　He inspects the whole place at a jog,
And he puts on great airs and fine antics galore,
While he chases the sheep till we're after his gore,
　Though he may be the Presbyt'ry Dog.

'Twas last Sunday a dog in the church went ahead
　With an ill-bred and loud monologue,
And the priest said some things that would shiver the dead,
And I'm with him in every last word that he said—
　Ah, but wait—'twas the Presbyt'ry Dog.

PATRICK CARROLL —                                    "THE PRESBYT'RY DOG"

# TANGMALANGALOO

The bishop sat in lordly state and purple cap sublime,
And galvanized the old bush church at Confirmation time;
And all the kids were mustered up from fifty miles around,
With Sunday clothes, and staring eyes, and ignorance profound.
Now was it fate, or was it grace, whereby they yarded too
An overgrown two-storey lad from Tangmalangaloo?

A hefty son of virgin soil, where nature has her fling,
And grows the trefoil three feet high and mats it in the spring;
Where mighty hills uplift their heads to pierce the welkin's rim,
And trees sprout up a hundred feet before they shoot a limb;
There everything is big and grand, and men are giants too—
But Christian Knowledge wilts, alas, at Tangmalangaloo.

The bishop summed the youngsters up, as bishops only can;
He cast a searching glance around, then fixed upon his man.
But glum and dumb and undismayed through every bout he sat;
He seemed to think that he was there, but wasn't sure of that.
The bishop gave a scornful look, as bishops sometimes do,
And glared right through the pagan in from Tangmalangaloo.

"Come, tell me, boy," his lordship said in crushing tones severe,
"Come, tell me why is Christmas Day the greatest of the year?
"How is it that around the world we celebrate that day
"And send a name upon a card to those who're far away?
"Why is it wandering ones return with smiles and greetings, too?"
A squall of knowledge hit the lad from Tangmalangaloo.

He gave a lurch which set a-shake the vases on the shelf,
He knocked the benches all askew, up-ending of himself.
And oh, how pleased his lordship was, and how he smiled to say,
"That's good, my boy. Come, tell me now; and what is Christmas
    Day?"
The ready answer bared a fact no bishop ever knew—
"It's the day before the races out at Tangmalangaloo."

# OWNERLESS

He comes when the gullies are wrapped in the gloaming
    And limelights are trained on the tops of the gums,
To stand at the sliprails, awaiting the homing
    Of one who marched off to the beat of the drums.

So handsome he looked in the puttees and khaki,
    Light-hearted he went like a youngster to play;
But why comes he never to speak to his Darkie,
    Around at the rails at the close of the day?

And why have the neighbours foregathered so gently,
    Their horses a-doze at the fence in a row?
And what are they talking of, softly, intently?
    And why are the women-folk lingering so?

One hand, soft and small, that so often caressed him,
    Was trembling just now as it fondled his head;
But what was that trickling warm drop that distressed him?
    And what were those heart-broken words that she said?

Ne'er brighter the paddocks that bushmen remember
    The green and the gold and the pink have displayed,
When Spring weaves a wreath for the brows of September,
    Enrobed like a queen, and a-blush like a maid.

The gums are a-shoot and the wattles a-cluster,
    The cattle are roaming the ranges astray;
But why are they late with the hunt and the muster?
    And why is the black horse unsaddled to-day?

Hard by at the station the training commences,
    In circles they're schooling the hacks for the shows;
The high-mettled hunters are sent at the fences,
    And satins and dapples the brushes disclose.

Sound-winded and fit and quite ready is Darkie,
    Impatient to strip for the sprint and the flight;
But what can be keeping the rider in khaki?
    And why does the silence hang heavy to-night?

Ah, surely he'll come, when the waiting is ended,
    To fly the stiff fences and take him in hand,
Blue-ribboned once more, and three-quarters extended,
    Hard-held for the cheers from the fence and the stand.

Still there on the cross-beam the saddle hangs idle,
    The cobweb around the loose stirrup is spun;
The rust's on the spurs, and the dust on the bridle,
    And gathering mould on the badges he won.

We'll take the old horse to the paddocks to-morrow,
    Where grasses are waving breast-high on the plain;
And there with the clean-skins we'll turn him in sorrow
    And muster him never, ah, never, again.

The bush bird will sing when the shadows are creeping
    A sweet plaintive note, soft and clear as a bell's—
Oh, would it might ring where the bush boy is sleeping,
    And colour his dreams by the far Dardanelles.

PATRICK CARROLL       "OWNERLESS"

# LAUGHING MARY

With cheeks that paled the rosy morn
  She bounded o'er the heather,
And romped with us among the corn
  When we were kids together.
Her mother's help, her mother's mate,
  Her mother's darling daughter,
When riper mind and more sedate
  The rapid years had brought her.
As pure as air from mountain snows,
  As dainty as a fairy,
As fetching as the native rose,
  And always—Laughing Mary.

A little mother round about,
  The happy sunshine bringing—
You'd see her bustle in and out,
  A-working and a-singing;
And then the soul of Casey's place,
  The love, the light, the laughter.
When friendship showed its cheery face,
  And music shook the rafter;
And many a lad went home to find
  A haunting sweet vagary
Was rambling softly through his mind
  Because of Laughing Mary.

But when the smiling stars were blurred,
  And someone's heart was bleeding,
She flew as flies the homing bird,
  With balms of comfort speeding.
An angel in a sweet disguise,
  She filled the measure over,
While tears stood sparkling in her eyes
  Like rain-drops on the clover;
And many a head bowed low to pray,
  Howe'er her skies might vary,
The years would bless her on her way
  And keep her Laughing Mary.

# FIRIN' ON THE EIGHT

He has his poky workshop at the far end of the town,
A shabby sort of pocket thing that's frail and tumbledown;
'Twill hold a one-twelve wheel-base, but if it measures more
The lamps are hard up to the wall—he cannot shut the door.
On the vacant block beside him are wrecked cars on the dump,
With thistles growing through the wheels and spiders in the sump;
And over all's the shingle, with the obvious written clear:
"Spare parts for every make of car. Chas Butson, Engineer".

You never see a job about except the old affair,
He drives for hire round the town in chronic disrepair.
She's had it, truly had it—still, she earns the bite and sup,
And while she waits outside the door the bonnet's always up,
While swallowed to the pockets, liquidated to his rear,
And tinkering with her innards is Chas Butson, Engineer.
An artist he in overalls with grease upon the same
So wastefully abundant you could tell the maker's name.
Withal he is a cheery soul and grins at passers-by,
Blacked out with grime and engine-oil save teeth and whites of eye;
As to the curt but friendly-meant, "How's things," he answers "Great—
Everything's in order, son, and firin' on the eight.

"Firin' on the eight of them, hittin' on the lot,
Never let the other fellow know she's not too hot.
Don't squeal about your troubles, always keep them out of sight
Beneath the little bonnet, son, and clip the bonnet tight.
There's no one interested, no one wants to hear you moan
About your private aches and pains—they want to tell their own.
You got to get your ups and downs, you got to hump the load,
The same as what you've got to face your punctures on the road;
You've got to get your issue, and you'll get it, don't forget,
So get them all together, get it over, then you're set.
That's common sense, now ain't it?—Wipe the whole thing off the slate,
Maintain your rubber healthy and keep firin' on the eight.

"Firin' on the eight of them and sparking fair and square,
A sticking piston now and then is neither here nor there;

You got to get your bother, that is fate, so there you are,
There's something wrong with every man and every motor-car.
And that don't go for common jobs the likes of me and you—
The jokers in the pricey class they get their troubles too;
They get them or they think they do: a nut that won't behave,
A knock they only think they hear which drives them to the grave,
A songbird in the body work which gets across their souls.
Ask the cove that drives the Cadillac, the guy that runs the Rolls—
There's something wrong with all of 'em, they're only human, see,
And they can do their big end in the same as you and me.
Then what's the use of fretting for a knock you can't locate,
So while you hang together, son, keep firin' on the eight.

"Firin' on the eight of 'em, ticking over nice,
A spot of bother now and then is always worth the price;
It keeps you sort of used to having everything go wrong,
And don't you just appreciate the break that comes along.
Here's me aboard the old 'un with snooty sort of fare
When phut she goes, shuts up, konks out ten miles from anywhere.
I'm tinkering here and tinkering there and tinkering out of luck
And listening to the silly cove inquiring am I stuck,
And giving out his crook advice: it's hard to take, but, see,
I never go the language more'n 'solutely necessary—
You can't get booked for thinking things 'twould never do to speak.
You feel inclined to scrap the junk and push it in the creek
With snooty underneath it, then you fluke upon the spot;
You never know just what you did, but bang! she's on the lot,
Firin' on the eight again, she's only got the four,
But eight it sounds more classy when you're talking motor-lore.

"So firin' on the eight she is and just touching forty-five
And pulling like a thirty horse, she's fun to be alive;
You never felt your heart so gay, your spirits half as bright,
The scenery is crack-a-jack and everything is right,
Half throttle out across the flats and coasting down the drop,
The boot shoved through the floorboard and she takes her hills on top.

PATRICK CARROLL —        "FIRIN' ON THE EIGHT"

You never knew her run so sweet—no, never, s'elp me bob—
With all she's got stuck into it and singing on the job.
'She's runnin' nice,' you tell the bloke, but all he does is grunt—
He ain't got the remotest of what's going on in front.

"Yes, half these coves who drive around they don't know what is what,
Three thousand sparks a minute, son, delivered on the dot.
Them's figures, ain't they? Spare me days, you don't know where you
　　are:
It's split split seconds split again that times a motor-car.
To blokes like them it's nuts and bolts and gears that make the whole;
Not on your life, for I maintain a motor's got a soul.
She's got a soul, too right she has, and, what is evident,
She's got the box of tricks they call a woman's temperament;
She's got the lot, and listen, boy, if I'd a singer's tongue
I'd sing the song of motor-car which no one yet has sung—
I'd pep it up a coupla thou, home polished on the note
With orchestra of moving parts that makes the motor mote.
See what I mean? Wha's that?—You're afraid you're running late;
I'm busy too meself. So long! But keep her on the eight."

# OLD SISTER PAUL

O Salutaris Hostia, the Alpha and the Omega
  Within the monstrance fair;
How sweet the maiden voices ring while to and fro the censers swing
  And incense fills the air.
A-down the convent chapel aisle the sisters kneeling filé and file
Show all that's noble, pure and good in radiant valiant womanhood.
  And where the shadows fall
There kneels a feeble silent nun whose useful working-day is done:
With human hopes and earthly needs, and so she tells her rosary beads—
  Old Sister Paul.

All wrinkle-seamed and bending low; and yet I mind long years ago
  At that same altar rail
I saw a group of maidens stand—no better, finer in the land—
  To ask the holy veil.
And worldlings wondered much that they should vow their fresh
    young lives away,
So dowered with every human grace, alert in mind and fair of face;
  And one whom I recall
Was first in poise and beauty—yes, and more than earthly loveliness—
  'Twas Sister Paul.

Tonight in her appointed place the shadows hide her weary face
  And fall across her heart;
And I have known what things, forsooth, have worn away the bloom
    of youth:
The treadmill grind from day to day—the hard exacting price they pay
  Who choose the better part.
A draughty schoolhouse long ago perched somewhere near the line of
    snow,
Or on the Plains where simmering heat had buckled every desk and
    seat
  And warped the timber wall
Through which the wind blew grit and grime on book and slate at
    lesson-time—
A dreary outpost blank and bare, the only brightness smiling there
  Was Sister Paul.

Her world a class of eight or ten; but purpose fired her pulses then
  And mantled on her cheek,
For all her ardent woman's love was drawn to serve her God above
  And succour here the weak.
But that's all counted with the past, and only Love survives at last.
The tapers stir tonight and flick a gem on vase and candle-stick,
And sparkle on the altar set, and dare to climb the gold lunette
To wave a twinkling bannerette
  Before the Lord of All.
The censer swings with rhythmic beat, the incense curls about His feet,
The organ trembles in His praise, while she her silent homage pays
As on her rosary's loom she weaves a lover's crown of autumn leaves—
  Old Sister Paul.

Oh, sweet the Sisters sing tonight, their soft true voices clear as light.
But down the lane of memory across the years there comes to me
  A tender children's hymn:
A simple thing in tune and words they sang as artless as the birds,
  Yet strong men's eyes grew dim.
The organ whispered tenderness beneath an artist hand's caress,
And here a voice would come anon to cap the pitch they faltered on,
While hushed folk hoped, and hoped in vain to hear that golden voice
    again;
  But Mary's praise was all
That stirred that full corrective note; and I have heard in years remote
Old people tell with phrase afire the wonder of that children's choir—
  And Sister Paul.

Her school's dismissed for many a day, the scholars scattered far away:
  They're changed and chastened now,
With grown-up cares that warp, and wreak the tell-tale wrinkle on the
    cheek
And thin the hair; but yet, to her they're still the bonny things they
    were
  With curls upon the brow.
Tonight with all their winsome ways they troop around her as she
    prays.

'Tis hers to guide their heedless feet on open road or city street,
So wheresoe'er they are,
Against their trespasses she pleads—defends them with her rosary beads,
And many a fervent Ave's said for that poor erring tousle-head
Whose steps have wandered far.
And I have seen him, at the last, redeem the squalid tragic past
  Before the curtain's fall:
He turned to pray; no prayer he had save one she taught him when a
  lad
Before his head was bowed with shame; and hot tears gathered at the
  name
  Of Sister Paul.

If books were balanced only here, such things as these would appear
  As "Sundries". This I know:
That He Who had the hundred sheep and left the ninety-nine to keep
Upon the track that tiresome day of one poor weakling gone astray
  Would not account it so.
The trampled corn, the smoking flax, the frail defeated melted-wax,
  The lost lamb's plaintive call
Were never scorned at Nazareth; and mercy is no shibboleth
To her who loves His bruised reeds and tracks them round her rosary
    beads—
  Old Sister Paul.

So while today the long hours through she gets the loose odd jobs to
    do—
She "takes" the convert, or with joy instructs the wayward backward
    boy,
  Or (but tell it not in Gath)
Outsits the tedious "sitter-on" who always seems to pick upon
The busiest hour to occupy the Reverend Mother's time, and try
  What self control she hath—
She questions not, for fair is fair, she makes it all a holy prayer.
  Nor need she care at all:
Bright blooms along the paths she trod are footprints on her way to
  God.

A veteran she, with duty done, and more, an ever faithful nun,
  Old Sister Paul.

Oh, "Adoremus Evermore" they sing; the Benediction's o'er,
The chapel empties pew by pew, the Sisters passing two and two.
  She moves to join the train,
But here where once with queenly grace, the morning freshness on her
    face,
She stepped His radiant chosen Bride, she falters now at eventide
  And genuflects in pain.
Still be it so, what's writ is writ; 'tis twilight and her lamp is lit
  Against the Bridegroom's call;
Oh, may the road she yet must meet lie easy to her tired feet;
'Tis but a step, for angels wait to welcome at the Eternal Gate
  Old Sister Paul.

# THE PARISH OF ST MEL'S

Beyond the vague wheel-tortured track
  The wandering mailman knows,
Away outback and further back
  And still outback it goes.

It's on the map with boundaries pat—
  The sure official touch—
A line that goes from this to that
  And connotes shires and such,
And longitude and latitude;
  But commonsense and guess,
The rainfall and the roving mood
  Have fixed its true address:

The fencer's camp, the shearing shed,
  The furthest trapper's tent,
Where human souls by fortune led
  Dry rot in banishment,
The straggling holdings scattered round,
  Drought-scourged, unhelped, decayed,
Where strong brave men selected ground
  And braver men have stayed.

The names of all of these you'll meet,
  From babe to patriarch,
Hard written on the census sheet
  With dash and question mark.
And many cherished names display
  A note recorded there:
"Have left the parish", "Gone away"—
  No inkling why or where.

You'll meet them scattered through the land,
  The young, the keen, the best,
To grasp the chance with open hand
  They never got Out West.

# THE DURKINS

Have you ever seen the Durkins at the Sunday morning Mass
  At the little old St Peter's week by week,
Since Old Man and Granny Durkin, then an Irish lad and lass,
  Made their home upon the farm along the creek?

There've been Durkins and more Durkins ranged sedately in a row,
  Thumbing prayer-books with the pictures through the text.
When the bench was filled with Durkins then the Durkin overflow
  Had to take up fresh allotments in the next.

Years ago came Old Man Durkin when the world and he were young,
  And the colleen wife he brought across the sea
With the dimples and the blushes and the brogue upon the tongue
  And a little Durkin cooing on her knee.

Then another, and another as the years went marching on
  And turned them into sturdy lad and lass,
But whatever were the changes, you could always count upon
  Another Durkin cooing at the Mass.

Faith, Old Man and Granny Durkin left a string of them behind,
  Splendid men and splendid women, loved and prized.
And the Durkins that came after kept the lesson well in mind
  Till St Peter's, so 'tis said, was Durkinized.

Yes, and some were Durkinesses, and they wouldn't be outshone,
  But of course they had to change the honoured name,
So we've Walshes and McCarthys and O'Connors, and so on,
  But we reckon them as Durkins just the same.

There are little toddling Durkins lisping sweet phonetic prayer,
  There are Durkins in the First Communion class,
There are Durkins for confirming, and as everyone's aware,
  There's a further Durkin cooing at the Mass.

Yes, the altar-boy's a Durkin, proper, pious and sedate,
  And the choir is mostly Durkin kith and kin,
While a sober-sided Durkin, faith, he takes around the plate,
  And it's Durkin, Durkin, Durkin putting in.

Now, then, hold your tongue a minute, I know what you're hinting
    at—
  'Tis that everyone's a Durkin but the priest.
You can leave that to the Sisters, for they all have noticed that,
  And their wonderment at such has never ceased.

Now they're making a novena that the Durkin altar-boy
  Will develop leanings that way; and if so
There could be no heavenly gesture which would bring a greater joy
  To a loyal band of mortals here below.

If the Bishop will ordain him in the little church out here
  There'll be Durkins!—ha-esh, it's looking far ahead,
But begobs I'd love to see it. See them come from far and near,
  I'll be looking forward to it though I'm dead.

Well, Old Man and Granny Durkin take their sleep in holy ground
  Where the Durkin plot is filling up, alas!
If a monument you're seeking, well, then, take a look around,
  Count the Durkins at the Sunday morning Mass.

# SING ME A SONG

Sing me a song with the ring of the truth in it,
Sing me a song with the freshness of youth in it,
Chant me a paean of joy;
I'm tired of the dirge with regrets and despair in it,
Life has too much of drab sorrow and care in it,
Raise me a chorus with hopefulness rare in it,
Plucked from the heart of a boy.

Give me the splash and the shout of the sea in it,
The trebles of birds and the bass of the bee in it:
Bring the spring's minstrels along,
Trilling a lay with the zest of young life in it,
Tender and clean with no heartache of strife in it:
Send me a message with joyfulness rife in it,
And the singer I'll love for the song.

# THE DAY TH' INSPECTOR COMES

It doesn't seem like school at all
The day th' Inspector comes;
You'd think the youngsters, big and small
Were shined up for a fancy ball—
Such fal-de-dal-de-dums;
There's shoes and frocks and stockings white,
And frizzy hair in ribbons bright
What's been tied up in rags all night,
And curly-wurly-ums.
We're all wound up and sitting tight,
The day th' Inspector comes.

We're not supposed to know what day
It is th' Inspector comes;
But Sister gets a ring to say,
"Brown paper parcel's on the way."
Then us and her is chums—
She hunts us round to try to make
Things decent for th' Inspector's sake;
You wouldn't believe what pains we take,
Nor how excitement hums;
We work with broom and mop and rake
Before th' Inspector comes.

The spiders gets it in the chest
The day th' Inspector comes;
The stupid boys they graft the best,
And down comes every hornet's nest
In smither-rither-rums;
And Sister says, "Boys, burn that mess."
There's filled-up exers. numberless,
And broken slates and canes, I guess,
What all your fingers numbs—
We jams the lot behind the press
Before th' Inspector comes.

We have the blackboards cleaned real hard
The day th' Inspector comes;
The fireplace is freshly tarred,
There's not a paper round the yard,
Nor crust of bread nor crumbs.
Inside's a table neat whereat
Is sticks of chalk and pencils pat,
A comfy chair, a bonzer mat,
And real geran-i-ums.
We only put on dog like that
The day th' Inspector comes.

He'd like to nip you in the stew
The very day he comes;
He thinks he's pretty cute, he do;
But Sister knows a thing or two
Outside kirriculums.
To ketch you on the hop's his whim,
But she has everything in trim;
So when he sneaks up sour and prim
To start his tantarums,
We're sitting up expecting him,
The day th' Inspector comes.

She sticks in front the kids that fag,
The day th' Inspector comes;
But coves like me that loaf and lag,
And other coves that play the wag,
Or has thick craniums,
We sit along the wall all day,
And get swelled heads to hear her say,
"That lot back there would turn you gray
Just mixem-gatherums."
The best ones always are away,
The day th' Inspector comes.

The Sister looks a bit knocked out
The day th' Inspector comes;
She has a headache and a pout,
But sticks to us without a doubt,
And in his ear she drums,
That we could really do the lot
Except the little bit we got;
But, golly, don't we get it hot,
Next day about the sums.
You'd think we didn't do a jot,
The day th' Inspector comes.

But this is where she does him brown,
The day th' Inspector comes.
While makes a smile replace a frown—
He holds the sewing upside down,
And haws and hems and hums;
She knows she has him beaten quite,
And crowds it on him left and right,
He handles it as if 'twould bite,
And don't we just enjoy the sight
The day th' Inspector comes.

Yes, school is not too bad at all
The day th' Inspector comes;
You sit up along the wall,
And don't let on you hear him call,
Keep playing hidey-hums;
But when he's gone with all he knows,
You feel like when the circus goes,
You come to school in shabby clothes,
No fril-de-dill-de-dums.
And you can thank for all your woes
The day th' Inspector comes.

But still we grin at all the jokes
The day th' Inspector comes;
It's great to hear him give some pokes,
Especially at the "clever" blokes
What gets mixed in their sums.
At all them little jokes we roar
And then he starts to crack some more—
He's cracked them fifty times before—
And them kinunderums.
We take him off behind the door,
The day th' Inspector comes.

They hadn't met for fifty years, or was it fifty-one?
They'd parted when their ship arrived their separate ways to run.
The old Baptismal Register back home in County Clare
Held both their names in faded ink, the same day written there.
Together in the parish school they conned the ABC,
Together, too, they went along to join the seminary.
Together in their long white albs with new-anointed hands
They took the yoke and sailed away to work in foreign lands;
Nor did they meet again till now, when, each upon his stick,
Two bony hands are gripped, and Father Pat meets Father Mick.
The spring and summer days have gone, the winter's nearly through,
Says Father Pat to Father Mick, "And here's long life to you."
Says Father Pat, "'Tis fifty years; and how the time has gone."
Says Father Mick, "I think you'll find it's nearer fifty-wan.

"And how's the world been treating you these many summers past?
You don't look one day older, man, than when I saw you last."
"That all depends," said Father Pat, "upon the point of view,
But thanks for them kind words, Mickeen, and here's respects to you.
And how is this and how is that? Now tell me have you heard
From those who took the step with us. I haven't had a word
At all at all, since we came out, from Mat or Tim or Con
These fifty years." Said Father Mick, "'Twill soon be fifty-wan."

But whether it was fifty-one or just the fifty neat
The time went by as time will do when after years we meet:
A kindly fairy flitted in to touch the past with gold,
And two old fogies gazing back forgot that they were old.
The Irish larks were in the skies, the Irish hills were green,
There came the smell of new-mown hay along the old boreen:
Old friends were met, old tales retold again and yet again—
"Ho, ho, begob," said Father Mick, "it was a grand world then."

And when at last the parting came and twitching fingers met,
It might have been the wintry breeze, but four old eyes were wet.
Said Father Pat to Father Mick, "A mighty treat it's been;
Now, can't we meet again, and soon? We're getting on, Mickeen—
The years are passing overhead, and passing dreadful quick;
Don't wait another fifty." "Fifty-wan," said Father Mick.

Well now, it's over forty years, the parish record tells,
Since I stepped out with fine ideas promoted to St Mel's.
A coming place, a rising town, the Bishop's letter read,
A stepping-stone by God's good grace to better things ahead.
Alas, for tips episcopal and barren seeds thus sown,
The stepping stopped the day I set a foot upon the stone.
I'm still just Father John today, though frankly I allow
There was a time I had my dreams—that's past and done with now.
I dreamt my young man's dreams indeed, that long before today,
My brilliant gifts all recognized. I'd be upon my way
To papal decorations and diocesan acclaim—
With red around the buttons, faith, and letters to the name.
But here we are this year of grace, the name Old Father John,
Who's shunted in the loop-line while the traffic passes on,
The signals all against him, forgotten, out of date,
Remembered by the Bishop only when returns are late.
The Consultors! did you mention them?—Ah, well now, what's the
    good;
An agreeable lot of nice poor fellows who would help you if they
    could.
No! No complaints, for, mind you, had the pickings come my way
With all they have to give I'd be a lonely man today
In the front seats of the mighty, looking bored or dignified,
In a kind of isolation with the Bishop at my side.
Instead of which I'm down the hall, a rabid unionist,
With my treasured friends still with me—all debating how we missed.
Well, that's the truth; and as for me I want no honours now,
No titles do I covet, for I have one anyhow:
They call me Father here around, and I have found it good;
The rich, the poor, the down and out all share that fatherhood;
A father to the thoughtless lad whose friends have been his foes,
The comely lass who cannot see beyond her powdered nose,
And in the dim-lit silent church each weekend over there

I'm Father to the erring ones who need a father's care.
And men of every creed and none they greet me with a will,
Except the perky bank-clerk who calls me Mister. Still,
I'm Father to the ninety-nine and I would have you know
I wouldn't swop that title, faith, for aught they could bestow.
Nor would I give this backward spot for all their fiddle-de-dee,
The ups and downs of forty years have made it dear to me.
I came here to a block of ground and many lonely weeks,
I batched it like a homeless tramp and foraged at the Greeks'.
From here I combed my parish wide on horseback day by day
Beyond the furthest settler's hut two hundred miles away;
But that was when the step was light and fire was in the blood,
I saw the way the tide was set and took it at the flood.
Look round you now a church and school and convent crown the hill,
And every stick was built by me and paid for—better still.
So when the Bishop makes his rounds with purpose in the face,
Upsetting all the usual calm decorum of the place
(The whole staff with the jitters; the housekeeper hits the roof,
The curate busy on the job and keeping well aloof),
I take him calm, produce the books, suppress all buts and ifs,
He'll find the whole transaction there—if versed in hieroglyphs.
And that's the point: says he to me, "Now, Father John, look here,
That way of keeping books has been outmoded many a year,
No balance struck but noughts and crosses up and down and littered in
    between
And no one but yourself and God can tell just what they mean."
They mean the wrinkle and the sear, the heartache in the night,
When no one lent a helping hand to aid me in the fight.
I scraped and begged and talked and bluffed, and when returns were
    thin
And bankers calling for their cut I put the savings in.
Then placed a cross to mark the spot where sleeps a heart's desire
To meet my ain folk once again around an Irish fire.

PATRICK CARROLL
"PASTOR OF ST JAMES"

But that is all beside the point: I started out to say
I wouldn't leave this nest for aught that's offering today.
There's ups and downs in every place, there's better and there's worse,
And distant hills are green and fair right round the universe.
Content's the thing; content is mine, I envy no man's lot,
But thank my God upon my knees for all the things I've got:
The finest people in the world—with tact and stratagem
I know that they'll put up with me and I'll put up with them.
And so I'd block the Bishop if he called on me to fill
The Vicar-General's parish, which of course he never will.
You might as well go try and shift that old gum-tree out there
And all its tangled roots disturb and plant them other where:
You'd only break its ageing heart, for it would pine to leave
The scene of happy sapling days and perhaps the birds would grieve.
To put that poetry into prose: I'm like that bent old tree,
And simple souls like little birds have placed their trust in me.
Old gnarled and rugged Father John, I've watched my people grow
Around me as the years went on; the records there will show
That I baptised them, married them, baptised their parents too.
I know their stories good and bad—the laurels and the rue.
I romped with them when they were babes and jumped them up in
    play
(Begob, you'd want a hoisting jack with some of them today).
What matter if at times I use the bitter word to strike—
I'm in this parish long enough to say just what I like.
I'm welcome, faith, to take my stand 'neath any Catholic roof,
And wag an inch below their nose the finger of reproof.
It's plain and blunt old Father John, I know the yarns they tell:
The takings off and goings on and, faith, they do me well—
There's fact and fiction woven through the yarns that they recall,
With ragged bits from *Comic Cuts* I never said at all.
Pernickety, that's what they say; ah, yerra, what's the use!

I barge and storm and blaze away and pitch them to the deuce;
'Tis all the love that guards the plant in him who toils and delves,
For I would give my heart's last drop to save them from themselves;
They know it and they understand and when the skies are grey
They come to me as children might to drive the clouds away.
When things are black and all has failed and every hope is gone,
Then someone says, "You go round and see old Father John."
I'm doctor, lawyer, arbiter and something more than that,
A conjurer who brings at will the rabbit from the hat.
I pull the strings and save the job and pay the rent that's due
And lend, of course, the "coupla pounds" to set them up anew.
'Tis not, of course, the modern touch, the ultra-streamlined way,
They've clubs and guilds and groups and things to do the like today.
I'm out of date, the Bishop says, and that he harps upon
He'll have his chance to pull the stack when I am dead and gone.
He'll send some smart young cleric here with notions brave and bold,
Who'll turn the whole place upside down, and that before I'm cold.
Good luck to him: the wheels must turn, new times new modes be-
    speak,
But for the nonce I carry on and use the old technique.
No style about the quiet old church where I officiate,
The wattle waves across the fence, a track leads to the gate;
And simple faith in simple hearts burns ever soft and bright,
Akin to that wee ruby lamp aglow by day and night.
No fuss, no pomp, no big days here—I've always baulked thereat;
I teach them how to say their prayers and if they'd stick to that,
Just say their prayers and trust their God and petty wrongs condone,
And understand another's rights are sacred as their own,
There'd be no need for all the hate where neighbours scowl and frown
And nations standing by their guns to shoot each other down.
Ah, yerra, what's the use of this tall talk and blatherskite,
It's just that I am balancing the vital books tonight.

There's something on the credit side I hope and trust to run
Against the fearsome debit of the things I might have done.
It won't be long before the few years left shall slip
And I must stand to answer for my faltering stewardship.
The hill is getting steeper now each day as I begin
To trudge home with the paper when the Sydney train comes in.
And people down the town I meet—I recollect the face
But never seem to strike the name, and say things out of place,
Forgetting things and muddling things, the memory moving slow,
But clear on little trifling things that happened years ago;
Old names come who fought with me the struggles of the past,
And those who rallied round me first are nearest at the last.
They're gone, all gone, they sleep tonight down there beneath the sky,
And my absolving hand it was that bade them all good-bye.
The street of unremembered men has claimed them one by one
We leave a feeble work behind when all is said and done.
I know the place, the plot, the row where each of them is laid
And soon I'll take my place—ah, well, I'm not at all afraid:
There's something on the credit side I hope and trust will run
Against the fearsome debit of the things I might have done.

PATRICK CARROLL